Wicked Decatur

The Transfer House in Decatur's Lincoln Square, 1906.

Wicked Decatur

TROY TAYLOR

THE History PRESS

Published by The History Press
Charleston, SC 29403
www.historypress.net

First published 2011

Manufactured in the United States

ISBN 978.1.60949.160.4

Library of Congress Cataloging-in-Publication Data

Taylor, Troy.
Wicked Decatur / Troy Taylor.
p. cm.
Includes bibliographical references.
ISBN 978-1-60949-160-4
1. Crime--Illinois--Decatur--History. 2. Murder--Illinois--Decatur--History. 3. Corruption--Illinois--Decatur--History. 4. Decatur (Ill.)--History. 5. Decatur (Ill.)--Social conditions. 6. Decatur (Ill.)--Biography. I. Title.
HV6795.D38T39 2011
364.109773'582--dc22
2011004525

We have it direct from the officers that the city is infested with large numbers of crooks, and we deem it wise that our citizens should be warned. The members of the fraternity that is now making life so hazardous are said to be the smoothest class of criminal lot. They are well dressed and from appearance would be the last of a class of men to be looked upon with suspicion. Every day, several of them come under the notice of the police. To bear out our remarks, we need only to post the astonishing number of hold-ups and other forms of robberies that have occurred in the city of late. From what has occurred of late, it is very evident that these bold sons of Barabbas are having their way in this man's town.

—*Editor of the* Decatur Bulletin-Sentinel, *December 28, 1895*

CONTENTS

ACKNOWLEDGEMENTS

I have many people to thank in Decatur for all the ways they have both helped and hindered me over the years as I have worked to chronicle the darker side of local history, from the crime era to the ghosts that haunted the city. While I can't list all of them here, I don't want to forget Skip and Sue Huston, Larry and Cheryl Haubner, Charley Barding, Haven Taylor, Tom and Cindy O'Dear, John Winterbauer, Adam White and others too numerous to list. I'd also like to thank my editor at The History Press, Ben Gibson, for continuing to put up with my oddities, and the readers who have tolerated one more book about Decatur. I promise this is the last one—I think.

CARVED OUT OF THE PRAIRIE

Decatur's Early Years

In 1854, Colonel Dan Conklin built a whiskey distillery, racetrack and whorehouse on the Illinois prairie, not far from Decatur. This earned the area the first of its unflattering nicknames: "Hell's Half Acre." Vice, and plenty of it, kept Conklin's establishment in operation for many years. Later, as is often the case with the criminal element, his descendants turned their attention to politics, and a Conklin was elected mayor in 1895, ushering in an era of corruption unlike anything the city had known before. This Conklin ran with only one idea in mind: bringing back the gambling that had been banned in the city a few years before. His campaign was heavily funded by local gamblers, and he easily won the election. Although gambling, along with liquor and prostitution, came and went as legal pursuits in Decatur for the next several decades, Conklin's short term in office truly brought about the reputation that has plagued Decatur for more than a century.

Hell's Half Acre may have been the region's first infamous nickname, but it would not be the last. By the 1910s and 1920s, the town of Decatur was referred to as the "Second Most Corrupt City in Illinois," gaining notoriety as a place where murder, bootlegging, prostitution, kidnapping, gambling and political corruption were common. It was during this time that my great-grandfather became a member of the Decatur Police Department, creating a connection between my family and crime in Decatur that still endures today.

Decatur started out as barely an idea on the Illinois frontier, a rough settlement that would likely never last. The first home built near the future town was a log cabin erected in 1820 by William Downing, a fur trapper and honey gatherer. Downing and his wife came from near Vandalia and remained until just 1824. His wife was afraid of the Indians in the area, so Downing sold the cabin to the John Ward family and took his wife back to civilization.

The Wards, a large Irish family, included Mary Ward and her seventeen children. Her husband, John Ward Sr., had died in Kentucky a few months before they came to Illinois. Mary's oldest son, also named John, died in 1831, but not before playing a prominent role in the founding of Decatur.

Leonard Stevens has been called the first permanent settler of Macon County, where Decatur is located, and he arrived in 1821 or 1822 with part of his family. They settled three miles north of present-day downtown Decatur on what is now called Stevens Creek. Other settlers soon arrived and began building homes near the Stevens settlement. Most of them were from eastern states like New York, Pennsylvania and Ohio, but the most notable exceptions were the Hanks brothers, John, William and Charles, who came from Kentucky and were cousins of Nancy Hanks Lincoln, mother of Abraham Lincoln.

As the Stevens settlement was growing, another settlement was building up near the Sangamon River, where the Ward family was living. These settlers came from the south, places like Tennessee, Kentucky and the Carolinas.

The two settlements thrived for several years, but then rivalry and dissension developed between them. The move to petition the Illinois legislature for the formation of a new county was handled by sending three men from the Ward settlement to Vandalia, at that time the state capital, to get authorization. The men succeeded in January 1829, and public meetings were held to select a site for the county seat of the new Macon County. At the meeting, several fistfights broke out between men from the Ward and Stevens settlements, and one man from the Stevens settlement was beaten so badly that he later died.

A site was selected north of the river, and Benjamin Austin, who had been selected as county surveyor, and his brother, William, platted out the village of Decatur. It was named after the naval hero Stephen Decatur, who was noted for his bravery during the wars with the Barbary pirates in the early 1800s. By the spring of 1834, Decatur boasted about eleven buildings, including some homes, two stores, a courthouse, a couple of taverns and a jail. The town began to attract new arrivals and new businesses, including a small store that was started by a Springfield firm called Bell & Tinsley. The firm sent a stock of goods and a young man name Hawley to act as a clerk. He soon tired of living on the frontier and returned to Springfield, which was far from a big city at the time—but it was better than Decatur, he said. The shop that he opened survived and became Decatur's first real mercantile store and post office. Mail was a luxury back then, and the first postmaster, William Cantrill, had little to do. He later became a county treasurer and a member of the state legislature. Cantrell Street (which was misspelled) on the city's East Side was named in his honor.

The Dewee brothers, Samuel, Joseph and William, started a store in the first brick house in Decatur on South Main Street. John Miller made the brick, and the Dewees, who were masons, did the brickwork. Miller's brickyard was located near present-day Fairview Park, but the early bricks were not exactly stable. When the city jail was constructed from these bricks, it was said that it "could be picked to pieces with a darning needle."

The city of Decatur had barely begun when it was almost wiped out during one of the first winters of its existence. Many settlers died from the extreme cold during the winter of 1830–31, when central Illinois was hit with disaster. This terrible season would be remembered for many years as the "Deep Snow."

Early that winter, following several torrential rainstorms, snow began to fall and continued to come in intervals, sometimes alternating with sleet and freezing rain. This treacherous mixture formed a layer of snow and ice that blanketed the state with frozen drifts that rose as high as six feet. Storms with high winds continued for sixty days. Many settlers who had depended on going into the nearby forest for firewood found themselves trapped in their homes. Travelers remained wherever they happened to be when the snow first started. Those who tried to continue their journeys often perished. One newspaper report told of "Cold Friday," when a man, his wife and their six children froze to death, huddled about their half-burned wagon on the prairie.

The snow drifted so high that loaded wagons could be driven over the top of fence rails. Livestock perished, and soon game became scarce. At first, the deer and other game became trapped in the snow and were easily caught, but as time wore on, they were eaten by the settlers and by wolves, causing the population to dwindle almost to nothing. It would be years before the squirrels and prairie chickens could be found to hunt again, and it has been said that the winter of the Deep Snow took the last of the buffalo from east of the Mississippi River. It was a calamitous season and one that would be remembered for many decades to come.

Many settlers died in the bitter cold and snow. Some people simply vanished, while others' remains were found when the snows finally melted with warmer weather. A lingering cold damaged the spring corn crop, game was scarce for years and the cotton fields in southern Illinois perished and never returned. When spring arrived, the snow and ice melted and turned creeks into impassable torrents. Cholera epidemics, caused by the wet conditions, sent many of the survivors of the Deep Snow into their graves.

Nature struck again in late 1836. Melting snow covered central Illinois with pools and lakes of slushy water. On December 20, an unseasonably warm day, a fast-moving arctic cold front sliced across the region, freezing the water solid in a matter of minutes. Anyone who was caught out in the open ran for shelter, and many of them didn't make it. Those unlucky souls, along with cattle, hogs and other animals, were frozen fast to the ground and died on the spot. One quick-thinking rider cut open his horse and crawled into the carcass to stay warm—unfortunately, he was later found inside it, frozen to death. One man, who was driving a herd of hogs to market when the cold front arrived, fled with his workers to safety, leaving the hogs to pile on top of one another for warmth. The animals on the bottom of the pile suffocated, while those on the outside froze, creating a pyramid of five hundred dead hogs.

Decatur survived the disastrous season and went on to become a center for commerce, railroads and crime on the Illinois prairie.

The first real businessman to settle in Decatur was William Warnick, who operated a tavern along the Sangamon River for several years. Warnick later became Macon County's first sheriff and, during this time, administered the only two horse-whippings that were officially recorded in the county. In 1832, he publicly whipped two horse thieves and received $3.50 each for the floggings. His sheriff's salary was $6.00, which was mostly earned by collecting taxes and attending the County Commissioner's Court. This meant that he earned a lot more money running his tavern than he did from his official duties.

Perhaps the most enterprising businessman of early Decatur was James "Uncle Jimmy" Renshaw, who started a tavern and store in October 1929. Renshaw was born in North Carolina in 1794 and moved to Kentucky, then to Illinois, where he married Sarah Phipps. They came to Decatur in 1829, and believing that the new town had good prospects, Renshaw erected the first real building within city limits, where he started his business. His tavern soon became the center of Decatur's social life.

Water Street, a hub of Decatur's business district, 1908.

Many residents visited Renshaw's store to buy whiskey and rum, but he also carried many other kinds of merchandise, including tools, medicines, clothing, cornmeal and assorted food items. The settlers rarely had money on hand, so Renshaw offered charge accounts and even cash loans on occasion. He soon prospered and invested most of his earnings in real estate. He laid out an addition in the northeast part of town, where he farmed for several years. He lived in a cabin on land now located in downtown Decatur and in 1859 replaced it with a brick house. Unfortunately, he died soon after from injuries he sustained while digging a well. Renshaw and his wife had six sons and two daughters, and when he died, he left them an estate of more than one thousand acres of land, including an orchard on the corner of Main and Prairie Streets.

Another of Decatur's leading businessmen, Silas Packard, came to town in a traditional covered wagon in 1830 and was one of seven children. His father died soon afterward, and Packard was left with the responsibility of providing for his mother and siblings. He went to work on a local farm, earning twenty-five cents a day, and in his spare time, he attended a subscription school by mail, as there were no public schools in Decatur at the time. He later became one of Decatur's first mail carriers.

Packard always had a yearning for travel, and the enterprising adventurer struck out for the gold fields of California in 1850. He stayed five years and made enough money to launch himself into business when he returned. He owned a lumberyard, a dry goods store and a streetcar company called the Decatur Electric Railway Company. He also was a banker for a short time. One of Packard's ventures was Riverside Park, which opened in 1890 and is remembered as one of Decatur's greatest attractions. The park was constructed along the Sangamon River, east of Maffit Street and south of Cantrell. It boasted swimming, boat rides, carnivals and even a log flume that shot passengers more than fifty feet down to the river. More than fifty boats could be rented, and there were steamships that took excursions up and down the Sangamon. Packard Street in Decatur is named in honor of Silas Packard.

Edward O. Smith came to Decatur in 1837 with just nineteen dollars in his pocket and went on to achieve great success as a building contractor during the years that followed. He erected a number of Decatur's most important buildings between 1860 and 1890. In 1847, he was elected to the Illinois Constitutional Convention and took an active part in drafting new laws for the state. He was later elected to the office of mayor and served Decatur during the Civil War. He was also elected to the Illinois Senate.

Smith had a leading role in bringing the railroads to Decatur, and if not for his efforts, the Illinois Central line would have bypassed Decatur altogether. The original plans had the tracks running about six miles west of the city, but thanks to Smith's lobbying and political influence, the route was changed.

In 1870, he built the Smith Opera House and then moved to California a short time afterward. He returned to Decatur many times over the next two decades, and when he died from heart failure in 1892, he was buried in the city that he helped to build.

Smith's greatest rival was Franklin Priest, another pioneer of Decatur. Priest came to Decatur in 1853 and operated a wide variety of businesses that included a sawmill, distillery, blacksmith shop, brickyard, tannery and general store. He also owned an omnibus line, a streetcar line, a hotel and dozens of parcels of real estate throughout Decatur. His sawmill made bridge timbers for the railroad, and the wood was constantly in demand as new lines and spurs were being built. He kept a group of employees working around the clock along the Sangamon River and at his center of operations around Franklin and Priest Streets (Priest Street was later renamed Decatur Street). His largest business venture was his general store, which was located on South Water Street. Priest kept all of his businesses centered on what was called the Old Square, now Lincoln Square, in downtown Decatur.

But Priest's many successes, and his attachment to the Old Square, did not come without a price, and he made many enemies and business rivals. The Old Square was the first major business district in the city, but Priest was opposed by a group of men, including James Stapp and E.O. Smith, who wanted to shift the main points of business to a more prosperous area called the New Square, located around Central Park. Priest was bitterly opposed to this and wanted to keep the center of business where it was.

When plans were laid out for Decatur in 1829, the Old Square was the center of the city, and all the streets radiated outward from it. Ten years later, Captain David L. Allen and Dr. Thomas H. Read, two men who would steer the direction of Decatur for years to come, arrived in the city. They started a number of profitable enterprises, but one of the most successful was the Macon House, a hotel that would later come to be known as the Revere House. The hotel was built around the New Square and became one of the finest and most popular in the area.

It was soon evident that Read and Allen were trying to draw business away from the Old Square. They were aided in their efforts by Dr. James Stapp, who, along with E.O. Smith, constructed Stapp's Row. This was a block of five stores located on the south side of Central Park. They were three stories tall, and at that time, they were the largest and finest retail businesses in Decatur.

Stapp's Row was the second location for the city's only bank, the Peddecord and Burrows Bank. Once the Stapp's Row stores opened, and with Decatur's only bank located there, the New Square took over most of the city's business. This was not hindered by the fact that Decatur's train station was located on the eastern side of downtown, and travelers coming to town had to pass through the New Square before going anywhere else. This usually made a traveler's first stop the popular Macon House.

The two squares became a serious problem for Decatur. Many city planners believe that even having one square in a city is too many, because

Stapp's Row was built near Central Park and became part of what was known as the New Square. This started a rivalry among Decatur businessmen that lasted for many years.

businesses are reluctant to leave it, but two squares tore the city apart. The rivalry between the two business factions became intense and spilled over into the political world. If the East Side named a candidate for mayor, then the West Side would support an opposing candidate, and so it went.

The Priest Hotel, owned and operated by Franklin Priest, and the St. Nicholas Hotel were built on the Old Square, and E.O. Smith countered by building the Smith Opera House on the new square. Now, with a bank, four busy stores and other attractions, the New Square dominated Decatur business throughout the 1860s.

But all of that changed in 1871 when a fire destroyed the Revere House. It was never rebuilt, and the surrounding businesses began to fade. One by one, they all moved out, circling closer to the Old Square, which would later be named for the late president. The businesses in the Old Square began to prosper once again, and the Priest, St. Nicholas and St. James Hotels flourished.

The area around the New Square became one of the seediest parts of the city. A number of gambling houses and brothels took up residence and would continue to dominate this area for many years to come. The city jail was located at the corner of Franklin and East Main Streets, making it convenient for police to round up suspects in the area.

Priest weathered the discord between the two business districts and was elected mayor of Decatur five times. He served on the city council three times and also became known as the founder of what came to be called

Merchant Street. He offered Merchant Street to Decatur as a city market in 1857, but the offer was refused thanks to opposition from the political powers behind the New Square. Their proposed city market would have stretched alongside North Main Street, so Priest moved one street over and started Merchant Street instead, relocating several of his stores there.

By 1883, Priest's business career was winding down. Several of his less profitable companies, including a woolen enterprise, closed down in that year, and a tragic downtown fire wiped out several of his buildings. He had always invested heavily and borrowed money, so when his businesses started to fail, it wiped him out. He died in 1890 and was laid to rest in Greenwood Cemetery. Ironically, two years later, one of his greatest business rivals, E.O. Smith, would be buried just a few feet away from him.

One of the city's oldest industries is the Mueller Company, which currently manufactures water and gas distribution devices and pressure control gauges. The company started in 1857, when Hieronymus Mueller opened a gun repair and machine shop on West Main Street. The coming of the Decatur

Hieronymus Mueller (second from left) in the Benz motor car that would result in his death, the first automobile fatality in American history.

Rolling Mill in 1870, which manufactured iron rails, created a demand for a city water system, and Mueller was appointed to the post of city plumber. The job involved tapping water mains and required shutting off water pressure and draining pipes. As Mueller worked, he ended up repeatedly getting soaked. This inconvenience resulted in his invention of a tapping machine that would make connections in the pipes without turning off the pressure. The device revolutionized the process and is still in worldwide use today. Mueller eventually opened a manufacturing plant, and his six sons carried on his operations in plants across the country.

In his later years, Mueller envisioned a bright future for the automobile. In 1895, he imported a Benz motor wagon from Germany when there were fewer than a dozen such vehicles in the United States. Mueller took out patents on automobile transmissions, steering columns and water-cooling devices and even an entire new car. He had blueprints for an automobile factory drawn up and planned to start construction when he died suddenly in 1900, the victim of a terrible accident. He was working on his car while smoking a cigar, and sparks from it fell into the gas tank, causing the fuel to explode. In just this way, Mueller became the first recorded automobile-related death in America.

In the latter part of the 1800s, Decatur saw the development of numerous and very diverse types of industries, from brickyards to cigar factories to farm equipment manufacturers. In later years, companies like Staley's, ADM, Firestone and Caterpillar would dominate the city, leaving many of the smaller enterprises that once flourished as distant memories. Many of the smaller companies that once thrived in Decatur, like carriage manufacturers and barrel makers, became outdated and forgotten. Others moved on to new locations or simply vanished.

Retail trade originally began in Decatur around the small taverns and mercantile stores that served the needs of settlers. The first major department store in the city was Linn and Scruggs, which started as a dry good business in 1869. W.H. Linn and W.R. Scruggs started the store as a one-room operation with plans to succeed by underselling the competition. Dubbed a "fly-by-night" operation by critics, no one thought that it would last a year. Ten years later, though, the store moved to the southeast corner of West Main and Water Streets, and there it survived two disastrous fires before moving to a location at Main and Prairie in 1924. Another company eventually acquired it in 1970. The company flourished for a century and became a staple of the Decatur economy.

Many other companies have come and gone over the years, including Morehouse & Wells, Block & Kuhl, Bachman Furniture and literally dozens of others that have faded away, done in by the decline of the downtown shopping district. Decatur once boasted businesses as diverse as the Hi-Flier Kite Factory, soft drink bottling plants, Crane and Perfect potato chip factories, Sunshine Dairy, a Piggly Wiggly supermarket, Tolly's and hundreds more that have been sadly lost and forgotten.

Farming also continued to be a major industry in central Illinois, and some innovative farm implements were created in Decatur, among them a corn sheller and a check row planter. Inventor Robert Faries came to Decatur in 1863 and worked in several machine shops before devising an invention that tied knots in check-rower wire used in corn planting. It was considered one of America's most important farm inventions in its day. Within a year, he had started the Faries Manufacturing Co., which specialized in soda fountains, restaurant fixtures and home electric and gas fixtures. He devised the wire machine in his modest basement workshop and was soon employing sixty-five workers in a building behind his home on Grand Avenue. In his later years, he devoted his life to photography and nature study and invented the Autoposean attachment for cameras. In 1910, he purchased Wilson Park as a nature preserve, and it was renamed Faries Park in his honor. His daughters later donated it to the city after his death in 1919.

Robert Faries was not the only inventor in Decatur's history. Other inventions that were created in the city included the slot machine (1897); burial slippers (1895); wire mats to prevent sailors from slipping on ships (1892); the Fly-Killer, a screen and wire device we now call a fly-swatter (1900); automatic grain scales for threshers, elevators and breweries (1882); the Caligraph typewriter (1880); the Gatling gun, which was invented by Richard Gatling while in Decatur on real estate business (1864); a beer cooler and keg-filling machine (1862); fare boxes for streetcars and buses (1912); and even a doll's head invented by Lucretia Sallee in 1865.

Many have forgotten the impact that Decatur has made on the history of America, and in some cases the world, but there can be no denying that the city earned a place of honor when it comes to ingenuity and hard work.

DEATH RIDES THE RAILS

Murder, Crime and Decatur's Railroads

One of the most important events in the history of early Decatur was the arrival of the first railroad train. It arrived on April 21, 1854, and came to a stop at the new Great Western Railroad Depot, which was located at the corner of Broadway and Cerro Gordo Street. Regular passenger service from Springfield began on May 8.

At the time the first train arrived, the station was located outside the city limits, but it wasn't long before Decatur began to expand northward along the tracks. The railroad soon brought prosperity to the city, linking it to outside markets and distant cities. However, building the lines into the city had been a formidable task. The original line from Springfield to Wyckle's Corners was completed ahead of schedule, but it would take some time before the line into the city was finished. The tracks had to be laid across Steven's Creek, which in those days was work all done by hand. The men used picks to loosen the ground in cuts to the west, and then dirt was shoveled into carts and pulled by a single horse to where the fill was being constructed.

Labor was hard to find for this backbreaking work, and builders used immigrants, who would work cheaply, for most railroad construction. There had been two separate crews at the Steven's Creek fill, one Irish and one German. One story had it that on a Saturday night after payday, the Irish workers got drunk and raided the German encampment, armed with shovels, picks and bare knuckles. It was reported (falsely, as it turned out)

A Wabash train departs from the Decatur station. In years past, dozens of passenger trains departed from Decatur every day.

that several of the German workers were killed during this brawl, so the sheriff organized a number of armed citizens to assist in arresting the Irish troublemakers. They later learned that no one had been killed in the fight, but regardless, a lot of inebriated Irishmen spent the night in jail.

The Great Western Railroad changed names several times over the years and eventually became part of the Norfolk & Western Railroad. In addition, there were many other rail services to Decatur, although the greatest of these were the Wabash and the Illinois Central.

The first Wabash roundhouse was built in Decatur in 1869. It had eight stalls. The Wabash shops were moved to Decatur in 1884, and operations in the city expanded rapidly. In 1907, the company constructed a railroad bridge across the Sangamon River east of town. A year later, it built a forty-two-stall roundhouse that could, along with the locomotive shops, service 490 engines. Nearly all of the repairs on Wabash steam locomotives were done in Decatur, as were the diesel engine repairs that came after the conversion from steam between 1949 and 1952.

In 1926, the Wabash office building was constructed on East Condit Street. It housed officials in the mechanical, telegraph and signal departments. Decatur became the hub of all the railroad's operations, which by 1925 had a peak employment of over thirty-five hundred workers, making it the largest employer in the city. The Wabash had its own bank, its own hospital, its own insurance company and even its own police force. It was a force to be reckoned with in Decatur for many years, but eventually the company died out, and the Wabash merged with Norfolk & Western in 1964. A heavy loss in passenger service was cited as the main reason for the merger, and most of the service was finally abandoned. At one point, at its peak, the Wabash Railroad operated twenty-five passenger trains out of Decatur every day.

The second rail service to come to the city was the Illinois Central, which arrived in October 1854. Some of its tracks had been laid before those of the Great Western, but financial difficulties kept construction from being completed. Promoters of the railroad had sought a land grant to help finance it, but getting through the legislative red tape took considerable time. In 1847, a bill was in Congress to get the needed authorization for a public domain land grant to finance the railroad. It was pushed through the Senate by Stephen Douglas and through the House by Abraham Lincoln. Assistance also came from Henry Clay, John C. Calhoun, Sam Houston and Jefferson Davis. The bill was finally passed after extensive vote trading by Douglas with southern senators and was signed by President Millard Fillmore in 1850. Permission was granted by the Illinois legislature to start laying track in February 1851.

Five acres of land were donated by Decatur businessman B.H. Cassell to the Illinois Central for a station, located at the point where the Great

Decatur's train stations; the Wabash is on the left, and the Illinois Central is on the right.

Western intersected the Illinois Central line. The Union Station was built in the summer of 1856, and this building served until 1903; by then, both companies had built their own stations. The old Union Station included the Central House Hotel, which offered sleeping quarters, offices and a dining room. Abraham Lincoln spent the night at the hotel while attending the Republican convention in Decatur in 1860.

The new Illinois Central Station was built in 1900, and it became the loading point for twenty-seven daily passenger trains. Decatur was once the main stop between Chicago and St. Louis, but eventually passenger service was discontinued, and the old station was razed in 1951, leaving only memories behind.

RAIL YARD MURDER AND MAYHEM

Decatur was one of the most important railroad hubs in the state of Illinois for nearly a century. Thousands of people came and went through the rail yards. They used the passenger service, crossed the tracks and labored in an industry that could often be hazardous, resulting in scores of deaths, dismemberments and accidents. In addition to this, however, crime often ran rampant. Over the years, there were dozens of attacks, assaults and robberies. Railroad men were often robbed and beaten by tramps and thieves who were passing through, and bandits frequently raided the freight cars. The Wabash Railroad had its own police force to patrol the area, but even these hardened detectives were not always able to prevent the crimes that occurred.

One of the best examples of success by Wabash detectives occurred in January 1910 when they routed a gang of thieves who had been stealing from railroad freight cars that had been left overnight in the yards. The first robbery took place in the summer of 1909, when more than $4,000 in silver was stolen from an unattended baggage car. More thefts followed, and pressure from railroad officials led to stakeouts in the yards, undercover operations and more. In the end, it turned out to be solid detective work that traced the disappearance of seven bolts of allkaline (a substance used for making cloth) to a boardinghouse on Sangamon Street. When police found two men in possession of the material, they stated that they had bought it from two young men named William Bunzel and George Virden and had no idea that it had been stolen. A short time later, the police tracked down Bunzel at the home of J.O. Finnegan on East Sangamon Street. He was taken into custody as he was walking out the front door and was quick to name his accomplices in the gang of thieves, including Virden, who was arrested at his home on East Prairie Street.

With two of the robbers in custody, it was a simple matter to learn the names of the other gang members. Wabash detective Dan Sullivan, along with officers Mays, Park and Besalke, arrested a couple of local hoodlums known as the Hackert brothers, who had often been in trouble with the law, but it wasn't until they picked up the Hackerts that they learned the identity of the gang's leader: J.O. Finnegan, an otherwise upstanding brakeman for the Wabash Railroad. Detectives had not wanted to consider that the robberies had been an inside job, but the evidence against Finnegan awaited them when they raided his house and discovered an assortment of loot stored in his basement. Everything else that had been stolen had long before been turned into cash. The brakeman had been able to easily learn which cars contained the most expensive items, and then he pointed them out to his confederates. All of the men involved received prison sentences for their parts in the crimes, and the string of boxcar robberies came to an end.

One of Decatur's many still-unsolved murders occurred in a bunk car on the Illinois Central line in May 1906. The car was parked at the Wood Street crossing and became the scene of what police called a "Dago revenge murder" when Marco "Mike" Vitale was slain while he slept. Vitale was a transient railroad worker who had come to Decatur with his cousin, Thomasa Utallo, to work as laborers for the Illinois Central. The Italian immigrant was popular and had a reputation as a hard worker. Vitale had been to Decatur several times before, usually keeping company with his cousin and other Italians who worked for the railroad.

On the night of Tuesday, May 22, Vitale and Utallo went to supper and then returned to the bunk car that was parked on the line at Wood Street. A bunk car was a boxcar that had been fitted with stacked beds. It could be transported up and down the line, where work was being done, and was commonly used by temporary laborers who didn't have much money or didn't want to spend their wages on a hotel.

What exactly happened next—and how or why Vitale ended up dead—remains a bit of mystery, but most of it was pieced together from the testimony of Utallo, who was locked up as a witness at the county jail the morning after the murder. Since he spoke very little English, a local Italian grocer dubbed "Banana Joe" was brought in to serve as a translator. Utallo explained that he and his cousin had returned to the bunk car, and a short time later, two strangers, also Italian, stopped by the car and asked if they could bunk down there for the night. Since there were several empty beds, Vitale and Utallo readily agreed. The newcomers took two bunks at the south end of the car, away from the cousins, who had beds at the north end. The four men played cards for a while, and then the light was put out and everyone went to bed. Utallo said there had been no disagreement between the men, and no money changed hands in the card game.

At some point, about 4:30 a.m., Utallo heard a loud cry in the darkness, and he recognized the voice as that of his cousin. He then heard the door of the bunk car slam open and saw the two strangers fleeing from the car. Vitale yelled, "I am stabbed! Go see the boss!" Vitale then lurched out of his bed and stumbled toward the door. As the wounded man leaned against the edge of the doorway, he suddenly lost his balance and fell to the ground outside. The police later found him where he had fallen, one arm under his head, lying still and not breathing. Vitale was in his underclothes and covered with blood. He had been stabbed once in the side with a thin, stiletto blade. The single thrust had pierced his heart.

Meanwhile, Utallo pulled on his pants and raced from the bunk car. He ran several blocks to the home of Dan McNamara, the cousins' supervisor, who called the police. Captain Dan Myers arrived a short time later, but Utallo was unable to say in which direction the strangers had gone. Telephone and telegram bulletins were sent out to the surrounding towns, offering the best description that Utallo could give, in hopes that the fleeing men might be stopped.

The police spoke to several other laborers in the surrounding area, including some carnival workers who were sleeping in another car that was parked near the crossing. They recalled seeing two Italians hanging around the area on Tuesday afternoon but didn't speak to them and paid little attention to what they were doing. They could offer no clues as to the identities of the killers.

Detectives searched the bunk car and found Vitale's clothing where he left it. His shirt had been rolled up and used as a pillow, and his trousers were hung over a chair. They searched his pockets and found ten dollars in small bills, as well as about sixty dollars in Utallo's pants, which had been left in plain sight. This seemed to rule out the idea of robbery as a motive for the murder. After speaking with Utallo the next morning, they also ruled out the idea that some argument had taken place during the card game or that the murder was motivated by bad feelings between Vitale and the two men. As far as the investigators could determine, Vitale had never met either of them before.

Captain Myers believed the murder was a vendetta, or revenge against Vitale for something that he had done in his past, perhaps even before coming to America. He had a number of letters in his belongings from Italy, all addressed to Vitale Marco di Vincenzo. Vitale had also been working in Terre Haute for a time, as well as in St. Louis and Decatur. The police believed that perhaps he had made an enemy during this time who might have wanted to seek revenge against him. Captain Myers was quoted as saying:

> *The Italians of one class are often a vengeful set and they will go to most any extremity to carry out their desire when it comes to revenge. So great is this feeling that sometimes the vendetta of the old country will follow them to their new home. I believe that the two strangers came to Decatur for the express purpose of killing Vitale.*

Whether it was a revenge killing or simply a robbery gone wrong was never discovered. The two Italian strangers vanished into the night and were never seen or heard from again. The murder of Marco Vitale remains unsolved.

ANOTHER RAILROAD YARD murder—and one of the most famous unsolved murders in Decatur history—was that of former city police chief Omer E. Davenport, who was brutally slain by two unknown men just north of the Wabash station in October 1935. At the time of his death, he was on duty as a special patrolman for the Wabash Railroad.

Major Omer Davenport was one of the city's most respected and well-liked men in 1935. He had distinguished himself in the military and had become the commanding officer of the 130th Infantry of the Illinois National Guard. After serving during World War I, he returned to Decatur and became the chief of police for three years. He was the youngest chief to ever serve, taking over the position at the age of twenty-six. Davenport left the police department in 1927 and became a special patrolman for the railroad. After surviving a war, he probably never imagined that this important, high-paying job would be the one that would lead to his death.

During the early morning hours of October 8, the Wabash passenger train No. 17 arrived in Decatur from Chicago, and Davenport was nearby as it pulled to a stop just west of Morgan Street. In the dim light, he saw two black men jump from the train and dodge behind a flagman's shack. Davenport started in their direction to investigate, but before he could get

Left: Omer E. Davenport.

Below: The area of railroad tracks west of the Wabash station where Omer Davenport was shot on the night of October 8, 1935.

very far, both men drew revolvers and began firing in his direction. One bullet struck Davenport in the left leg, just above the knee, and the other passed through his neck, grazing his windpipe. He fell beside the tracks, bleeding heavily, while the two men fled in the opposite direction.

Noah W. Deyton, the fireman on train No. 17, was the only witness to the shooting. He told the police:

> *I saw two Negroes hanging around the shanty. When Officer Davenport walked down to the engine, looked at the tank and turned toward the shanty, I did not know he had seen the men. He started to walk around the shanty, and the two Negroes stepped back and started around, keeping the shanty between themselves and the officer. Then Mr. Davenport got out his flashlight, and as he walked around in front of them, both began shooting and Officer Davenport fell. Several men ran to him and he was taken to the hospital. The two Negroes ran south toward Cerro Gordo Street. I was too far west of the crossing to tell whether they turned on reaching the street or kept on going south.*

Railroad patrol officers began searching the area, and the Decatur police force joined in the hunt. Unfortunately, the description of the two men was sketchy, but the police had other clues to work with. The gun that killed Davenport had been stolen earlier that night from the home of Isaiah "Doc" Taylor, a black man employed at the Wabash roundhouse. Several items of clothing that had also been stolen were found on the ground near the watchman's shack.

Police detectives searched the area, and officers from throughout the city and county worked overtime on the case. The night shift worked all the way through the next day as they scoured the city for leads. The local highways, railroad yards and freight cars were searched, and one group of officers walked along the line from the Wabash yard to Elwin in hopes that some lead might be found. Trains were stopped and cars searched. Trucks were stopped on the highways, and deputies went to nearby towns to search the railroad depots. The state police aided in the search and broadcast the description of the suspects throughout Illinois.

Meanwhile, Omer Davenport had been rushed to the nearby Wabash Employees Hospital, which was located on East Grand Avenue, a short distance from the station. He was still alive when he arrived there but began to fail a short time later. The doctors, who initially felt that he might recover, began to offer a poor prognosis. The bullet that had struck his throat had

The Wabash Employees Hospital where Omer Davenport died.

worked itself into one of his lungs. It had caused serious complications, and if they tried to operate, they were convinced that it would kill him. He died later that night.

A few days later, the manhunt began to slow down. Detectives traveled as far as St. Louis and Chicago in pursuit of some sort of lead, but they found nothing. A reward was offered by the railroad in exchange for information about the killers, but it was never paid. Whoever the two men were, they vanished into history, leaving behind no clues as to their identities.

LAW AND DISORDER

History of the Decatur Police Department

The first law enforcement officer in Macon County was William Warnick. According to the few early records that remain, he found little crime in the area in 1829. One of the most exciting events to take place during his time in office was his whipping of two horse thieves in the public square in 1832. However, despite the claims of a law-abiding public in early Decatur, the second official building to be constructed there was a jail. It was a log building situated at the corner of Prairie and Water Streets. No records remain as to who was actually incarcerated there.

Decatur's first marshal was Captain John Hartley, who served from 1856 to 1857. He was a Mexican War veteran who later served in the Civil War. Although few records detail the enforcement of the law during this period, it is known that the marshal and his deputies were not the only ones maintaining law and order. Another group was the Anti-Horse Thief Association, one of the many vigilante groups that operated in Central Illinois.

The records of the police department in the middle and late 1800s are thin and, in many cases, nonexistent, but we do know that by 1876, the department had a marshal, deputy marshal and five officers. In this same year, the officers began wearing uniforms on their patrols. In 1882, a state law forced the police marshals to be appointed by city mayors, and Decatur's head official became the police chief. By 1900, Decatur's twelve officers were also appointed by the mayor. They worked seven days a week on twelve-hour shifts, and if any of them was ill, he had to find his own replacement.

Most of the information about the department from that time period comes from old newspaper reports. In the 1870s, most of the arrests in town were of vagrants and drunks, with occasional raids on houses of prostitution. The operators of bordellos, as well as the customers arrested in them, were usually fined three dollars, plus court costs. On many occasions, they were released with a "promise to pay" if they did not have enough money for the fine at the time of their arrest.

The police force operated with fairly primitive methods. It had one patrol wagon, a rogue's gallery of pictures and arrest records and a burglar alarm that was connected to all the city banks and some of the major business establishments. The patrol wagon had been incorporated in 1896 and was known locally as the "Kelly Wagon." It was named for a petty thief named Kelly who had lifted a wallet from a visiting minister at the fairgrounds. He became the wagon's first passenger.

Before the city had a jail with enough cells to accommodate drunks and other minor offenders, there was a "calaboose," or detention cell, in every ward in the city. Later, in the early 1900s, the city established the Short Street Holdover, a temporary jail, on the Levee. Offenders could be locked up there to sober up or to await the wagon that would take them to the main jail on the morning after their arrest.

During the late 1800s, the police force was still a fairly disorganized department and was often made up of men who were as rough and violent as the criminals they had been hired to arrest. Occasional scandals sullied the ranks of the men in uniform, like the arrest of Officer William Mehan in 1893. He was indicted for assaulting a man named Felix McKown in a bar fight. Mehan was only a part-time officer. He divided his time between the official police force and his job as a merchant policeman on the Levee. Merchant policemen were often hired by the legitimate merchants in town to look after their interests, especially in high crime areas and vice districts like the Levee. One night, Mehan was drinking after he got off duty and took exception to a remark made by McKown. He beat the man badly and was arrested and then indicted by a grand jury. He was eventually convicted, suspended from the police department for thirty days and fined six dollars. He came through the scandal with his reputation unscathed and in fact was admired by the merchants on the Levee, who wanted a man working for them whom the criminals saw as dangerous.

Things began to improve in 1899 with the appointment of Chief Ben Applegate, who had been a popular Wabash Railroad detective. He ordered new uniforms and star-shaped badges for his men and also began the undercover bureau, which patrolled in plainclothes in the depots and in the downtown areas at night. He also began rotating the foot patrols among the officers. There were already rumors of corruption and graft making the rounds, and Applegate believed that by moving the men to different areas on a regular basis, he could combat the problem.

In 1902, former police captain "Big Dan" Sullivan took over as chief. His major challenge while in office was a smallpox epidemic that led to the construction of a "pest house" and a "shoot-to-kill" quarantine for anyone caught leaving it. He was a popular leader among the men but was run out of office in 1905 thanks to a change in mayors. He was followed by P.K. Albert, a former patrolman who had once been a U.S. marshal in the Oklahoma Territory. Albert was also a victim of political squabbles involving gambling, vice and liquor violations. This was a time period when Decatur gained a reputation for being a wide-open town. Gambling had been banned in the city in the mid-1890s, but officials who were supported by the gambling interests were voted into office, and in return they reversed the laws. Decatur also attempted a ban on liquor in the early 1900s, but this, too, was reversed by the "wets" in April 1910.

Chief Roy Bendure was appointed in 1909 and continued the plan of cleaning up the department and the city. He began heavy enforcement of the local gambling and vice laws and conducted the city's first raid on an opium den, on Merchant Street, in November 1909. But like the officials before him, Bendure had problems with city leaders who were backed by gambling and vice interests.

In January 1910, city officials dismissed night sergeant Amos Imboden and night patrolman Frank Vording for "general incompetency." Another officer was demoted from sergeant to patrolman. Newspapers noted that whenever a man was removed from the force, the mayor's office gave no details other than to cite the cause as incompetency. However, rumor had it that Chief Bendure feared there were leaks in the department, perhaps paid for by the liquor interests. At that time, alcohol was prohibited within the city limits, and a short time before Imboden and Vording were fired, a major liquor raid was botched because the bootleggers had been warned in advance that the police were coming. Bendure was convinced that someone had been paid off. There were also numerous problems with gambling houses in the city, and it was common knowledge that at least fifteen informal casinos were permanently established and operating openly, even though it was against the law at the time. Bendure's hands had been tied by corrupt city officials when it came to raiding these establishments. These officials made a show of removing ineffective officers from the police force and giving Bendure the authority to close down gambling houses; it turned out to all be an attempt to garner good publicity in the newspapers. Chief Bendure eventually left Decatur and opened a detective agency in Kansas City, where he became nationally known.

In January 1911, another police scandal intrigued the city when Night Captain Kolp accused Day Sergeant Somerville of trying to discredit him with regard to arrests at several bawdyhouses and the disappearance of envelopes of cash at the city jail. Kolp had been accused of irregularities, but he insisted in the newspapers, and to the mayor, that blame actually lay with Police Chief Roberts and his friend Sergeant Somerville. Kolp stated that over a period of several months, the police had raided houses of prostitution in the city and arrested the occupants. Then, Chief Roberts rounded up the vagrants who had been arrested in the city and sent them to the now-empty bawdyhouses. The police raided the houses again and charged the operators with prostitution—then offered to let them off for a small fine, which was pocketed by the officers involved. Kolp was accused of planning these phony raids and taking the money, but he swore that he was innocent. The situation also involved accusations that Kolp had signed phony warrants in the case of a woman who was being followed by a private detective so that her husband could get information about her alleged affair. The Decatur Police Department became mired in this scandal after an Officer Whitehead and the woman's husband, Charles Lee, found her with a man named Murphy in a hotel room in Clinton. The entire situation was eventually sorted out, but it did nothing to enhance the reputation of the department.

In 1911, Decatur changed to a commissioner form of government, and this had a devastating effect on the quality of local law enforcement. Now, a city commissioner became responsible for appointing the chief of police and the members of the police force. Soon, under-the-table arrangements were being made to get men onto the force as favors for politicians and businessmen. In addition, jobs as police officers were awarded to those who would go easy on gambling parlors and bawdyhouses. Because of this, the police chief was often stuck with drunks, gamblers and corrupt men on the force.

The first Decatur policeman to be killed on duty was Carl Besalski, who was shot to death in the Wabash rail yards on August 8, 1912. He surprised a man named Andrew Rowan, who was sleeping in a boxcar, and Rowan shot him. Rowan received a life sentence for the murder. Public donations of more than $1,000 were gathered for the Besalski family, and Mrs. Besalski became the leader of a campaign to establish a tax-supported police pension fund. She was the first beneficiary of the fund when it was finally established in 1915.

One of Decatur's most corrupt periods extended through Prohibition in the 1920s and into the middle and late 1930s. A number of police officers were involved in liquor violations and were accused of accepting payoffs from bootleggers, gamblers and vice operators. Decatur's chief of police was even indicted in 1936.

In 1930, though, Decatur police carried out one of the most spectacular raids in the city's history, capturing a gang of bandits that had been terrorizing central Illinois for weeks. The heavily armed band of robbers was holed up in two houses at 709 and 717 Oakland Court and had fortified the hideouts with an arsenal of weapons, including machine guns, Springfield rifles and an assortment of handguns. The two houses each faced Oakland Court, but from different directions, and machine guns had been placed at strategic spots in both houses to protect the gang members from assaults.

The gang's series of robberies began on April 9 in Strasburg, Illinois, and this was followed by nine more robberies over the course of the next two weeks. Decatur police officers were tipped off to the presence of the gang by a Charleston man, who recognized one of the gang members driving through town. He followed the driver to the house at 709 Oakland Court. He immediately contacted the police, who set up a stakeout at the address. Over the course of the next two nights, officers observed several cars coming and going at the two houses and noted the presence of seven men and one woman, all going back and forth between the two addresses. The houses both had thick foundations, rising about six feet from the ground level, and each could be entered by both the front and back doors. The garages were situated to offer a straight run to the streets, one leading through Lincoln Park and the other through a residential area to Route 10.

On April 19, at 1:30 a.m., ten police officers and three Wabash Railroad detectives, all armed with machine guns, shotguns and rifles, raided the house. They arrived in several cars, roaring down the street and approaching both houses at the same time. They squealed to a halt, blocking the garage entrances, and the officers jumped out, guns in hand. The cars were left running, and men with machine guns took up position at the corner of both cars, covering the entire front of the house. Two other officers were dispatched to the rear of the houses, preventing escape from that direction. The other officers, moving as quickly as possible since the high foundations and windows of the houses offered a distinct advantage to the gang, went to the front doors.

Deputy Sheriff Belcher, accompanied by officers Goodwin, Gibbons and Perkins, went to the door of 709 Oakland Court, and Belcher pounded on the door with his fist. A man inside opened the door just slightly, and Belcher threw his full weight against it, knocking the man to the floor. With the other officers close behind, he pushed his way into the house. Directly in front of him, in the kitchen, were three men seated at a table, drinking and eating sandwiches. One of the gang members, Edward Miller, ran to the door of an adjoining bedroom, but Belcher stood in his path. "Your gun's not there," he told Miller. "It's better to come out of here without bullet holes in your hide." Miller surrendered, and the police later learned that the adjoining bedroom was the location of the gang's arsenal.

With the other men covered by the lawmen's guns, a fourth man who was lying on a cot in the front room with an automatic under his pillow, awakened to find himself handcuffed before he had any idea of what was happening. Without a shot being fired, the anticipated battle had come to an end.

At the same time that Belcher was raiding the house at 709 Oakland Court, Deputy Adeyelott and his men were capturing the prisoners at number 717. The only injury sustained was a bruise that one of the Wabash detectives received on his shoulder when he broke open the front door. The second house was just as cramped and small as the first, and the officers found the robbers sleeping on mattresses that had been dragged into the front room. In addition to weapons, the officers found an assortment of liquor bottles and jugs of home brew, as well as hacksaws, keys for all makes of automobiles, knives and "jimmy bars." The men were all arrested, and a woman who was with them was taken into custody by Mrs. Peniwell, the police matron.

The raid was widely publicized and was considered an important one by police officials. The officers considered themselves fortunate that no bloodshed had occurred. The gang didn't share their relief. "You're damned lucky," Edward Miller said to Deputy Belcher after the robbers had been taken to jail. "If that buddy of mine hadn't moved the shotgun, you'd be stretched out on a cooling board by now. Maybe both of us would."

Miller, who was described by the officers as a "hard guy," evidently meant what he said, for under further questioning, he told Belcher that he had been in prison and would rather be dead than be locked up again. He added, "I wouldn't hesitate a second to kill you. You took me by surprise, and not a one of us had any idea that officers were near. I'm not sorry for what we done—only sorry that I couldn't get to my gun."

An identification department was developed in the police department in the late 1920s, and starting in 1931 Lieutenant Steven Wood expanded the operation. Every prisoner suspected of a serious offense, as well as any suspicious characters who were arrested, were fingerprinted and photographed. In 1937, Wood also started the Decatur Investigation Bureau, which would be rated one of the best in the state. By the 1940s, the department had expanded further and began operating with eight squad cars, all equipped with modern radios, five motorcycles, forty-six call boxes that were scattered throughout the city and an armory that included Thompson submachine guns and tear gas.

In 1959, city government changed again and gained a city council and manager. For the first time, a chief was appointed from outside the department, and James H. May took over the job. He was a former police chief of Great Bend, Kansas, and Galesburg, Illinois. He immediately organized the department into three bureaus: Investigations, Patrol and Traffic. He also instituted an auxiliary police program and created a manual containing policy and (ironically, as it turned out) ethical procedures for all personnel. In 1967, May was indicted for official misconduct when it was found that he had been taking police evidence, including cash and weapons, for his personal use.

The police department has expanded many times in the past four decades and has managed, for quite some time, to avoid the scandals and embarrassments of the past. Today, the department faces a whole new array of crime problems—problems that could not have been imagined when Sheriff William Warnick was whipping horse thieves in the public square—but the majority of the force remains committed to the safety and protection of the people of Decatur.

"IF YOU CAN'T FIND A DRINK, YOU'RE NOT TRYING HARD ENOUGH!"

Prohibition in Decatur

When the Eighteenth Amendment to the Constitution, which abolished the sale and distribution of alcohol, took effect on January 16, 1920, many believed that it would cure America's social ills. Little did they know at the time, but it would actually do just the opposite. America's great thirst for forbidden liquor bred corruption in every corner. Law enforcement officials became open to bribes because the majority of them just did not believe in the law, but worse yet, Prohibition gave birth to the great days of organized crime. The gangsters of America had previously concerned themselves with acts of violence, racketeering and prostitution, but the huge profits that came with the sale of illegal liquor built criminal empires.

Prohibition did not come quickly to America. It took a long, hard fight before the "dries" had their way and imposed the well-intentioned but misguided legislation upon the country. Drink was a powerful and well-entrenched part of American culture, and one could find beer, imported rum or locally made liquor and cider in almost every frontier household. Everyone, young and old, drank it. A pitcher of beer was often found on the family supper table simply because the local water was usually unfit to drink. Alcohol was a basic ingredient in most old medicinal remedies, and many mothers put a cranky baby to sleep by adding a few drops of whiskey to his milk. When neighbors got together to raise barns, harvest crops or merely socialize, there were always jugs of whiskey on the table next to the platters of food.

In spite of this, there were those who felt that alcohol was evil. There were early, localized attempts at prohibition. Small towns, cities and counties all over the country tried, and often failed, to prohibit alcohol. In cases where the sale of alcohol was successfully banned, it was easy for residents to travel over the county line, or to the next town, for a drink.

Alcohol began to gain its questionable reputation with the coming of the nineteenth century. As the country expanded and immigration increased, there was a rise in the consumption of hard liquor as opposed to beer and wine. While many white settlers saw nothing wrong with using alcohol to cheat and demoralize the Native Americans, the more conscientious took issue with this practice. Evidence also started to emerge that showed alcohol, once thought to have numerous medicinal qualities, could also be hazardous to one's health. Few stopped to consider that it was overindulgence that was the problem, not general consumption.

An influx of lager-drinking German immigrants in the mid-1800s brought about a revival in beer consumption. American brewers began taking advantage of the new railroads to open up chains of taverns across the country in which they could sell their own brands. Saloons sprang up on every street corner in the cities, while small towns with one church and one schoolhouse might have a dozen or more saloons in their midst. With competition high, bar owners wanted to keep the booze flowing as much as possible and resorted to sidewalk hawkers and free (well-salted) lunches to entice men into their establishments. While some of the saloons were clean, respectable spots, many were dirty eyesores, operating on a shoestring budget, and were hangouts for bums, thieves and prostitutes. The opponents of alcohol needed no further evidence that liquor was causing the moral decay of the country.

Alarm over the increase in drunkenness, along with the growing political power of brewing and distilling companies, led to an increase in activity for the prohibition movement. The American Temperance Society was founded in 1826, the Women's Christian Temperance Union in 1874 and the Anti-Saloon League in 1892. These were only three of the many organizations dedicated to a total ban on alcohol. To gain more attention, and greater political leverage, these groups often joined with other, more worthy causes, like the abolition of slavery or a woman's right to vote.

The prohibitionists did not believe in moderation. You either did not drink, or if you did, you were doomed to damnation along with the gamblers, heathens, fornicators and godless foreigners. Female temperance fighters marched with banners that were emblazoned with slogans like, "Lips that touch liquor will never touch ours." Preachers claimed that the "wine" that

Jesus and his apostles drank was in reality grape juice and ranted about the dangers of drinking, which they insisted included blindness, insanity, poverty and children born sickly, already addicted to the devil's brew. They plastered walls with posters of bartenders (actually demons in disguise) serving tankards of draft, hopeless drunks staring in despair at empty liquor bottles and ragged children standing despondently outside the doors to taverns while inside their fathers were drinking away the grocery money. They dragged derelicts out of gutters and put them on display as examples of what alcohol could do to a man.

The "wets," those opposed to prohibition, made the mistake of ridiculing the prohibitionists instead of taking them seriously. Their jokes were no defense against the self-righteous solemnity of the movement. It was not long before state after state, and finally the entire country, adopted Prohibition.

The Volstead Act, which brought about national Prohibition in America, went into effect in 1920 and lasted until 1933. It stopped the manufacture, transportation, importation and sale of alcoholic beverages. The making of small amounts of home-brewed beer and wine for personal consumption was permitted, and stores selling home-brewing equipment and supplies sprang up everywhere. Many of them did most of their business with bootleggers. Medicinal alcohol could be purchased at a pharmacy with a doctor's prescription, a loophole that many doctors and pharmacists exploited until the government took steps to close it. The only alcoholic beverage that could be legally sold was "near beer," which had such a low alcoholic content that most drinkers didn't consider it worth the trouble, especially when the real thing was available from the friendly neighborhood bootlegger.

Today, we can look back at the advocates of Prohibition and call them naïve and misguided. We can also say that many of the politicians who supported them were hypocrites who were primarily interested in getting votes. However, the majority of the prohibitionists sincerely believed their cause was just and that the movement would solve America's problems. They believed that people would have more money to spend; crime rates would fall so drastically that police forces could be trimmed down to the bare minimum and jails and prisons could be closed down; poverty would be abolished; corn and grain that had been "wasted" on making alcohol could be used to feed the hungry at home and overseas; and men who once staggered home from the saloon on a Saturday night would now be up bright and early on Sunday morning to take their wives and children to church. It seems like wishful thinking to us now, but to the prohibitionists of the day, it was a bright vision for the future.

But, of course, Prohibition didn't stop anyone from drinking. In fact, it made drinking even more popular, simply because it was forbidden. Across the country, more than 200,000 speakeasies opened. These drinking establishments were so named because many of them were located behind, above or below legitimate businesses, and patrons often drank in silence to avoid detection. Huge bootlegging operations sprang into existence to supply the speakeasies and those who chose to ignore Prohibition. Disrespect for the law became the fashion as people who would never before have dreamed of doing anything illegal were now serving illicit liquor in their homes or drinking in the neighborhood speakeasy.

By outlawing alcohol, the authorities made criminals out of millions of otherwise law-abiding citizens. They seriously undermined the respect those people had for law and order, and worst of all, they offered the criminal underworld the chance to make more money than it ever dreamed possible. All of the money that had been made by robbery, prostitution, loansharking, bookmaking, extortion and other criminal pursuits was nothing compared to the windfall of bootlegging. Organized crime that was syndicated on a national, corporate scale was born and became so powerful that it has never been shut down.

Prohibition was widely considered to be doomed by 1928, but it hung on for another five years before it was repealed in 1933. By then, it had taken its toll. The court systems had become clogged; the jails and prisons were filled, often with people who had never been in trouble with the law before; trusted politicians, officials and police officers had been corrupted; and millions of dollars had been spent hiring new Prohibition agents, coast guard officers and cops. The drunken violence associated with seedy bars was nothing compared to the bloodshed that erupted in city streets as bootleggers battled for control of the liquor trade. By 1933, law enforcement was in disarray, and organized crime, which had grown bloated on the money from illegal alcohol, was so powerful that it could move onto other pursuits, like legalized gambling, with wide public approval.

PROHIBITION IN DECATUR, as in most American cities, was a complete failure. The people of the city had always been in favor of selling—and especially consuming—alcohol. Decatur had previously passed two laws to ban liquor sales, but neither had lasted for long. The longest-running alcohol ban in Decatur occurred in the early 1900s, during one of the city's short-lived "crime cleanups." There were a number of arrests and raids that took place

Millions of gallons of liquor and beer were seized and destroyed during the Prohibition era.

during this period, although enforcement was half-hearted at best. Many of the saloons that had been in Decatur for years were turned into "soft drink" parlors, supposedly offering only nonalcoholic refreshments. Not surprisingly, most of them continued to serve alcohol in the basement or in back rooms, which led to raids and arrests. The newspapers complained that it was nearly impossible to find jurors to serve during bootleggers' trials because the law was so unpopular.

As the 1910 election approached, proponents for the "wets" began lobbying for the liquor ban to be overturned. A number of local saloon owners and brewers started what was called the East End Club at 541 Short Street. It was started on the second floor of a building on the Levee and was outfitted with card tables and chairs. Members of the club were able

People lined up to drink in Decatur's "soft drink" parlors, just as they did in other speakeasies around the country.

to drink free beer that was supplied to them by F.H. Behling, a local agent for the Leicy Brewing Company. Since the beer was not being sold, the 250 club members were free to drink as much as they liked. The newspapers correctly pointed out that the club had been formed for political purposes, and the members were working to influence the upcoming election. They succeeded, and the "wets" were voted into office. The liquor ban in Decatur ended on May 5, 1910.

When Prohibition started on a national level in 1920, the popular outlook in Decatur wavered between completely ignoring the law and taking an occasional drink. Lawbreakers and suppliers were occasionally caught, but enforcement of the law was lackluster. Local bootleggers found that by spreading a few dollars in the right direction, they could ensure their booze shipments reached their destinations and guard against arrest at the same time.

In April 1925, deputy sheriff J.F. Mientkler and former police chief C.W. Crump were ordered by a judge to replace twenty quarts of Canadian whiskey that had gone missing while it was in their custody. The whiskey had been evidence in the case of an accused bootlegger, and when it was learned that the two officers were unable to account for it, the case was dismissed.

In May 1927, a recent recruit to the Decatur police department, Jack Loeb, was arrested during a raid on a brothel located at 135 East Eldorado Street. It was not until after he was booked and fined that his identity was learned—much to the dismay of Chief E.F. Wills. However, the chief quickly offered an explanation, claiming that Loeb, an inexperienced new hire to the force, had been sent out undercover to the brothel to see if they were selling liquor. Chief Wills added, "I told him of a few places where I thought he might be successful, and he was free to get evidence anywhere that he could find it." The chief did not explain how he knew where to find liquor and why nothing had been done to close those places down.

Decatur's shoddy enforcement of the Prohibition laws was known not only locally but also as far away as Washington, D.C. In fact, Decatur's arrest record was so bad that opponents of the law who were trying get it reversed used the city as an example before the U.S. Senate as proof that Prohibition did not work. At one point, Decatur's record of liquor-related arrests was the lowest in the nation.

Prohibition finally ended in 1933, and the story made newspaper headlines in Decatur. Many of the local taverns had already been stocked and were prepared to open on April 7, the first day for beer sales. On that day, over twenty-five hundred cases were sold in a matter of hours. Newspaper reporters interviewed people on the street, who were in the midst of celebration. "Now that legal beer is here," one of them said, "there isn't half as much fun in drinking it as there was when you might get arrested at any minute."

ROLLING THE BONES

Gambling in Decatur

Gambling arrived in the city along with the first taverns. It flourished through most of the 1800s before finally being banned in the latter part of the century. Those who made a living off gambling revenues were as disgruntled about the ban as the saloonkeepers were during Decatur's two short-lived liquor bans. Many of the gambling dens continued to operate despite police raids in 1895.

In early January, the police raided a room located over Allsburg's Saloon at 615 North Water Street. Marshall Lehman had received tips about the gambling parlor and decided to raid the place on a Sunday afternoon, when he heard that a game was going on. He sent several officers to the rear door and took several others with him up the main stairway. Lehman listened at the door for a moment, and when he heard voices inside, he knocked quietly. The door was opened and revealed a number of men playing poker and participating in games of chance. At the sight of the police, the occupants of the room scrambled to escape, but seven of them were taken into custody. Lehman questioned them as to the whereabouts of the owner, a man identified as R.G. Spence, and was told that he had stepped out but would be back soon. All of the men arrested had to come up with twenty-five-dollar bonds for their appearance in court as inmates of a gambling room and were released. Lehman and two officers waited in the room for the return of the owner, and in a few minutes, Spence walked back in. Needless to say, he was surprised to find the police in his establishment but paid a thirty-five-dollar bond without argument and watched as the officers confiscated the contents of the room.

Later in the month, the Decatur City Council met and passed another resolution against gambling, forcing Marshall Lehman to continue his raids. Council members complained that a number of gambling parlors were still operating in Decatur and nothing was being done to shut them down. On Monday, January 21, 1895, Lehman took a party of officers with him and began systematically closing every gambling parlor that he knew was operating in the city. No arrests were made and no fines levied, but Lehman ordered every parlor to close and to stay closed. Opinions varied about how strictly the new ban would be enforced. Many of the gamblers believed that the new rules were serious, and others felt that they were simply to appease members of the public who had been calling for the elimination of all gambling in the city.

The ban lasted only as long as the mayoral election that came in April 1895. With the election of Daniel Conklin as Decatur's mayor, a new era of vice was ushered into the city. Conklin was heavily supported by the gamblers in town, who managed to rally votes and raise money for his campaign. After the election, the gambling ban was lifted. Conklin's administration was mired in corruption, and rumors of payoffs and questionable police appointments were rampant. The city council rebelled in every way it could, even running council meetings without him present. State's attorney C.M. Lane refused to back off against the gambling syndicate in the city and was finally forced out of office in July. As a private attorney, he continued his fight and was later charged with criminal libel in November 1895.

Conklin's administration turned out to be short-lived, but the effects of it were felt in Decatur for many years to come. Gambling was eventually banned again, although it still flourished quite openly after the turn of the century. Police officials stated that gambling was taking place in almost every saloon in the city, but even after putting the establishments on a watch list, there was little they could do to stop it. Decatur had become a refuge for gamblers who had been driven out of other parts of the state, including Chicago, and the situation was now taxing the efforts of the local police force.

Gambling continued to be a problem into the 1930s. Officials in city government, and in the police department, were often criticized for looking the other way. At one point, concerned citizens even hired three Decatur attorneys to assist them in taking action against Mayor Charles Shilling because they believed he was doing nothing to stop the spread of gambling.

A Chicago private detective was hired to gather evidence to obtain search warrants that could be served on known gambling halls. Five search warrants were obtained, but the gamblers were tipped off, and nothing was found but empty rooms. Finally, the state's attorney was pressured into filing charges against the mayor, but he was later acquitted.

More search warrants were obtained, and this time the gamblers had no warning. The police seized roulette wheels, poker tables, cards and numerous other gambling devices at five different establishments. However, all five of the operators were later acquitted of gambling charges. Critics complained that the trials had been fixed. Meanwhile, gambling continued unhindered in Decatur.

Conditions worsened, and reports stated that the entire third floor at the south end of Merchant Street was occupied by Gordon Smith's horse-betting and craps parlor. In addition, the Denz Building, which was located in the same block, was taken over by gamblers Charles and Ed Lichtenberger for their operation. They had the windows boarded up or painted over, and the establishments were busy around the clock with customers, mostly men, of all ages and races.

One of the most famous gambling spots in Decatur was Emmett Byers's place at 124 East Wood Street. It was perhaps the most notorious of all of the parlors, boasting horse betting, cards, games of chance, craps and more, all within a block of the police station and the county courthouse. Byers had a number of brushes with the law over the years, including arrests for bootlegging and gambling. He operated one of Decatur's most upscale gambling establishments, the Lakeside Club, which was said to be the best-equipped casino in Macon County. The basement of the building was set up as a gambling operation with two craps tables, a roulette wheel and slot machines.

The Lakeside Club was just one of Decatur's upscale gambling and nightspots in the 1930s. The other was Caroline's Club. The city's elite could often be found at either of these clubs, which were technically outside the reach of the law as they were beyond city limits. Both offered dining and dancing, along with an array of gambling activities. The proprietors of Caroline's were Caroline and Peter Knudsen. They ran a quiet establishment with fine food, gambling and high prices. A local gambler and "colorful figure" named Harry Stewart ran the gambling operation there. He was rumored to be connected to crime organizations in the Chicago area. At one time or another, he was in some way involved with most of the major gambling operations in the Decatur area, either as a partner or manager or as "protection."

War between Decatur's gambling operations, reportedly influenced by the Chicago mob, began in 1929 with the attempted murder of Emmett Byers. About 11:00 p.m. on the night of July 9, a man who was unknown to the occupants of Byers's club came in and opened fire on Byers, wounding him in the ankle. The man fled, as did two carloads of Byers's customers. A neighbor called the police after hearing shouting and gunfire, but when officers arrived, Byers was not there. They eventually tracked him down at St. Mary's Hospital, where his wound was being treated. He refused to speak with police about the shooting.

In September 1931, a dynamite bomb was thrown into a gambling parlor owned by Elmer Cavanaugh at 248 North Park Street. The building was badly damaged, but no one was injured. A short time later, another bombing occurred, this time at a gambling parlor run by Jerry Manuel at the southeast corner of Lincoln Square. A wrapped packet of dynamite was thrown through the window of the establishment, and Manuel picked it up and tried to throw it down the stairs. The bomb went off in his hands, and he was seriously injured.

In February 1932, a robbery occurred at Lichtenberger's booking shop, which was located on the third floor of the Denz Building on Merchant Street. It was a steady operation that catered to businessmen, laborers and farmers and made a lot of money, making it attractive to anyone who wanted to get rid of the competition. Charles and Ed Lichtenberger had received several letters demanding that protection money be paid, but they had ignored them. No suspects were ever identified in the robbery, despite eyewitness testimony from several farmers in the gambling parlor and a cabdriver who was outside.

According to their accounts, a front man had entered the shop several hours before the robbery. He had taken a seat in the back of the room and had placed a few bets while he waited. About 6:00 p.m., seven armed men wearing goggles had entered the parlor, wrecked the place and made off with about $2,500 and a diamond ring. If they had struck just a short time earlier, they would have taken several thousand more dollars since the day's receipts had been taken out just minutes before.

The thieves disappeared into the night and were never captured. The Lichtenbergers saw it as a warning to close down the operation or face further consequences. They decided to temporarily close up shop, moving out the ticker machine and turning off the telephones. Word circulated throughout the city that business was being conducted on the street if anyone was interested, but for now, the Lichtenbergers were too nervous to set up in a new location.

The Denz Building on downtown Decatur's Merchant Street. In the fall of 1932, a bomb was exploded in the Lichtenberger's gambling shop, which had been set up in the building.

Time passed without incident, and a few months later, the Lichtenbergers reopened in another building. By the fall of 1932, they had returned to the Denz Building. They had ignored the earlier warnings, and on October 30, the booking shop was bombed. A black powder charge was set off in the stairway leading up to the gambling parlor. The force of the explosion was sent upwards, destroying the Lichtenbergers' operations on the third floor, blowing apart the stairway and shattering all the windows on the second and third floors of the building. Luckily, no one was injured in the blast. There were no witnesses to report who had placed the bomb, and of course, the crime went unsolved.

The Lichtenbergers, and many of the smaller operators in Decatur, closed up shop. Raids were conducted throughout the city in the days following the bombing, but no suspects were ever found. With so many operators out of business, it looked as though gambling in the city was finally on its way out. This proved to be only temporary. Within a few weeks, the booking shops and gambling parlors were again operating at full strength.

Gambling really did not come to an end in Decatur until about 1936, when the police finally stepped up raids on the local betting parlors and gambling, confiscating and destroying slot machines and gambling tables and arresting and fining the customers and owners. In the past, a police raid on a gambling parlor ensured that the place would be safe for a time before it was raided again. This was not the case in 1936 and 1937, however, as police continued to raid the same establishments over and over again, knowing that eventually the losses would drive the operators out of business, or at least out of Decatur. Apparently, this system worked, and most operators abandoned the city, hoping to find better luck elsewhere.

DECATUR

Kidnapping Central

Throughout the late 1800s and into the years of Prohibition, Decatur earned great notoriety throughout the Midwest. This sordid reputation was not one that city leaders of today care to recall, but at one time, the city was known to gangsters and lawbreakers as the perfect place to hide out from the law. Centrally located between Chicago and St. Louis, Decatur had so many methods of transportation to offer and boasted such an array of gambling parlors, cheap hotels and houses of ill repute that it was simple for just about anyone to disappear.

In addition, Decatur was frequently used as a hiding place for kidnap victims from the Midwest during the early 1930s. Local and state police became convinced of this fact and even believed that the kidnappers were using a particular location (which was never named in public records) northwest of the city as a drop-off point and hideout. It was said to be sparsely populated but in an easily accessible area where the kidnappers could come and go without being seen. Allegedly, the police were never able to obtain a search warrant at the location because they lacked actual evidence of any crimes.

Decatur was an ideal location, thanks to railroad and highway access, and was plagued by a largely ineffective police force. Hampered by corrupt officials at city hall, the hands of the department were tied when it came to prosecuting gamblers, bootleggers, brothel owners and kidnappers. Although crime often ran rampant, Decatur did not have a powerful underground, which could have offered problems for outsiders. The Chicago police long suspected that something was amiss in the city. Their suspicions arose over a period of several years when, time after time, baffled by a kidnapping in their city, they found all of their leads pointing south to Decatur.

An abducted millionaire from Monroe, Wisconsin, who was kidnapped in Chicago, was discovered in Decatur soon after his ransom was paid. He was found wandering the downtown streets in confusion, a short distance from the county courthouse. After a Kansas City beer baron was kidnapped and then murdered in 1931, detectives traced the gun that killed him to Decatur. The gun had been sold to the owner of a store in the Levee, who in turn sold it to a local criminal.

On January 13, 1932, two Chicago businessmen, H.D. Gentry and W.T. Fostch, were kidnapped in Decatur, tied up, robbed and then left on the side of a country road near Illiopolis as the kidnappers drove away in Gentry's Buick sedan. The two men were in the 200 block of West Eldorado Street at 12:15 a.m. when they were confronted by two men with guns. They climbed into Gentry's car and ordered him to drive west on Route 10. A second car, which contained three or four other men, followed close behind. After passing Illiopolis, the bandits ordered Gentry to stop the car.

The two businessmen were taken out into a field and robbed at gunpoint. They gave up about seventy dollars and their wristwatches, and then they were tied up with heavy cord. The men were marched into a coal shed on the edge of an isolated road and left there. They heard the motor of Gentry's sedan as the kidnappers drove away.

The men waited in the darkness for more than an hour as Gentry worked to loosen his ropes. Once he succeeded, he freed Fostch, and the two started back toward Decatur. They arrived at the police station about 6:00 a.m., exhausted from the experience and covered with mud. They briefly told their story to Sergeant Tim Collins and then went to their hotel to sleep for a few hours before returning to the station to give Chief Wills a more detailed account of the incident. As it turned out, it didn't do much good. The kidnappers were never caught, and Gentry's automobile was never recovered.

DECATUR'S VICE DISTRICTS

During the late 1800s and all the way up to the 1950s, vice districts catered to the illicit needs of any customers who cared to visit them. Usually located in areas that were easily accessible by the railroad, which made them popular with soldiers, vice areas were often seen as being borderline legal by the local authorities. Many believed that by segregating liquor, gambling and sporting houses in a central area, it kept these illegitimate activities from spreading throughout the entire city.

Decatur boasted a number of vice districts during the heyday of crime in the city.

Park Street

When the original plans were laid out for Decatur in 1829, the city was designed with a square at the center, with main streets radiating out in four directions. It was natural that the first businesses in the city were located at this site. However, when the Macon House—later known as the Revere House—was built at the southeast corner of Prairie and Franklin Streets, everything about Decatur business changed.

The hotel was the joint venture of two brothers-in-law, Captain David Allen and Dr. Thomas Read. Each friend had married the other's sister and had come to Decatur between 1828 and 1830. Each invested in real estate and began developing the East Side of the city. They built homes that became the cultural and social centers of the town and started a number of businesses.

The Macon House became known throughout the state as the finest hotel in the city. It soon became evident that Allen, Read and other businessmen on the East Side were trying to draw business away from the original town square, which was soon dubbed the Old Square. This push was strongly assisted by Dr. James Stapp, who settled in Decatur in 1855. Together with E.O. Smith, another early contractor, Stapp built Stapp's Row, a block of store buildings along the south side of the city park and close to the Macon House.

Prior to the construction of Stapp's Row, the city park was a grassy area that was overgrown with hazelnut bushes and infested with snakes. As more businesses gravitated to the area, the park was cleaned up and soon began to be called the New Square to differentiate it from the original square at the conjunction of main streets. More businesses followed, along with the city's only bank at the time, and it looked as though the New Square was going to become the dominant business district in the city. This was helped by the fact that the railroad depots were on the East Side of town, and travelers had to pass through the New Square to get anywhere else in the city. The first stop from the rail station was the Macon House, which made it the city's most popular hotel.

The two squares were a problem in the city for many years. There were serious conflicts, both financial and political, but the New Square began to fade after the destruction of the Revere House by fire in 1871. It was not rebuilt, and the nearby stores and businesses began to suffer. One by one, they closed down or moved away, no longer attracting visitors from the railroad stations. Businesses in the Old Square were quick to seize on the opportunity afforded by the loss of Revere House. The St. Nicholas became the city's leading hotel, and other hotels, stores and restaurants also began to prosper.

The area around the city park, Park Street and North Franklin became one of the seediest parts of the city in the late 1800s. Saloons moved into the spaces once occupied by stores and restaurants, and gambling dens and brothels followed soon after. The bars and taverns dominated the area for many years, creating a sordid history that has been all but forgotten over time.

Newspaper accounts reported on a dance that was taking place at a South Park Street tavern in 1891 that ended in a free-for-all fight. About 9:30 p.m., a saloon keeper named Julie Blackburn went to the police station at Franklin and East Main Streets and informed the officers on duty that a fight was going on at his bar. Blackburn stated that he had been beaten by Lee Hall, Harry Cooper and another man named Smith. Blackburn had marks on his face, several cuts and a variety of bruises. Officers accompanied him back to the saloon, but by the time they arrived, the place had cleared out. With none of his assailants around, the police arrested Blackburn and charged him with disturbing the peace.

In March 1894, two men, Andy Deppe and Cloyd Wood, got into an argument over a seventeen-year-old girl whom they had both been seeing. She worked at one of the saloons on South Park Street, and the two men ran into one another there. Wood was already at the bar when Deppe arrived. They stayed in the saloon for a little while and talked, and then Deppe called Wood out into the street. As soon as they stepped out, Deppe pulled a revolver from his coat and fired it point blank into the other man's face. The bullet barely grazed the ear of the intended victim and chipped a nearby brick wall. "God damn you, how do you like that?" Deppe roared at Wood. "I'll kill you yet!" He turned and ran away, and the crime was not reported until the next day. Deppe was arrested at the saloon where he worked on the Levee and was charged with attempted murder.

On January 27, 1895, Charles Spears was stabbed twice on Park Street. That afternoon, he had been at the Salvation Army barracks and had run into a man he knew named Charles Cavanaugh. He suggested that the two of them get a drink, and they went to John McAully's place on South Park Street. Spears admitted to having several beers, and while he claimed that he was not drunk, he got into an argument with the bartender after refusing to pay for drinks for several other men in the bar. They claimed that Spears had offered to buy them beers, but Spears denied this. He and Cavanaugh left the bar and started walking west toward Water Street, looking for another bar to visit. They had only walked a short distance before several of the men from the bar came out after them. They called out, demanding again that Spears make good on his offer to pay for their drinks. Spears turned around and saw one of the men taking off his overcoat, as though preparing to throw a punch at him. He walked toward the men, and one of them swore at him; Spears took a swing at him. According to Spears's story, three or four of the men jumped on him at the same time. He was badly beaten and stabbed twice, once in the shoulder and once just above his abdomen. He survived the attack and likely avoided Park Street for some time to come.

A more amusing incident occurred in a South Park Street saloon in February 1895. Police Officer Cross was called into the tavern to settle a disturbance caused by a young man named Charles Davis who was refusing to pay for three drinks. Davis told the officer that he had no money and offered to let him search him and see. Cross went through his pockets and found no money, but he did find some other interesting things. Among them were a .22-caliber revolver, a pair of handcuffs, two detective badges, a membership card for the Grauman Detective Agency of Cincinnati, Ohio, and several dime novels. Officer Cross took him to jail and charged him with carrying a concealed weapon and impersonating a police officer. When Cross asked him to explain what he was doing with the items, Davis said that he had paid a fee to join the detective agency and believed this gave him the right to carry the gun and badges. Davis also told him, showing him the books in his pockets, that he had read every adventure story written about secret agent Nick Carter and just wanted to help the police in fighting crime.

In June 1895, a broken-down, disease-ridden former bricklayer named "Happy Jack" Williams committed suicide in Robinson's Saloon on South Park Street, where he occasionally helped out. At the time, the saloon was empty, except for bartender Al Hay, who was sleeping. Robinson, the tavern's owner, was sitting outside. Williams was sweeping the floor and walked behind the bar, where Robinson kept a revolver. He picked it up, walked to the back of the saloon and sat down in a chair. Without a word, he raised the weapon and fired a bullet into his head. It entered his right ear and exited his head just above the left temple. At the sound of the shot, Robinson and a number of others who had been sitting in front of the saloon ran inside and found Williams slumped over in his chair. The smoking revolver was still in his hand. Williams's body was taken to the Brintlinger undertaking establishment and prepared for burial. Robinson paid for his funeral and expressed regret over Williams's death. Illness had prohibited the man from working for many years, and out of sympathy, Robinson offered him a job and a place to sleep in the room above the tavern. He told the newspaper that Williams had never spoken of taking his own life, but the saloonkeeper said he was not surprised that he had.

In time, the saloon district around Park Street faded away. As downtown Decatur cleaned up and new businesses pushed toward the city park from Water Street, the seedy taverns and gambling parlors moved on to other parts of the city.

MERCHANT STREET

Merchant Street was started in downtown Decatur by Franklin Priest, one of the most enterprising businessmen in Decatur's history. The street was located on land that Priest owned next to North Main Street and just steps away from Lincoln Square. Because the piece of property would make a street that was only one block long, he offered it to the city for the site of a farmers' market. The offer was refused, however, thanks to opposition from the political powers behind the New Square. They knew that if the city market were located near the Old Square, this would draw many visitors and farmers to the area, theoretically damaging business in the New Square. With the proposal denied, Priest started Merchant Street instead, and he moved several of his stores and businesses there. Other businesses followed, and soon there were banks, stores, restaurants and real estate offices lining both sides of the short street.

After the Revere House burned down in 1871, more businesses came to Merchant Street and the area around Lincoln Square. For the next dozen years or so, Merchant Street continued to prosper, but at some point, for unknown reasons, it began to draw a criminal element. As one legitimate business closed, or moved to another location, a tavern or gambling parlor would take its place. Merchant Street began to become an island of crime at the edge of the thriving business district, and from the 1880s through the 1930s, it was regarded as one of the most dangerous places in Decatur.

The Lichtenbergers' gambling operation, which was bombed in 1932, was located on Merchant Street. Other vices thrived here as well, including prostitution, liquor and narcotics. The first raid on an opium den took place on Merchant Street in November 1909.

On the afternoon of November 5, Officer Brant observed a number of African American people entering a stairway that led to the second floor of a building at the south end of Merchant Street. He went into the business on the ground floor and could hear people upstairs making a lot of noise. He telephoned for assistance, and two other officers joined him. The three men forced their way into the rooms on the second floor. As they searched the place, they found not only liquor (which was illegal at the time) but also a large quantity of opium and numerous pipes and bowls. The ten black occupants of the den were arrested after scattering in terror at the sight of the police. One woman, Hattie Watkins, was found hiding in an icebox with a sack over her head. A patrol wagon transported them to the city jail. The newspaper noted:

> *The opium outfit is the same kind used in the Chinese opium dens of San Francisco and other cities with large Chinese populations. There were three or four extra bowls, many pipes, a little lamp used for lighting the pipes, the little steel rods used for filling the pipes and stirring the "dope," and quantities of opium.*

Some of the earliest reports of vice on Merchant Street come from June 1883. A man named Joseph Taylor was arrested and fined for keeping a house of prostitution in the back room of the third story of an old bank building on Merchant Street. His daughter, Sarah Taylor, and several other women were also arrested and had to either pay a fine or leave town.

In August 1889, the police department announced that it was "declaring war" on streetwalkers and prostitutes in the city. On the night of August 12, police raided several locations on Merchant Street, including the upper floor of Keister's Saloon, where they arrested three Decatur women and a young girl from Monticello. The newspaper commented, "It is the well-founded opinion of officials that Decatur has more than her share of streetwalkers without importing them from Monticello."

"George Hunt is a well-known character about town," the *Decatur Daily Republican* noted in January 1895, "and when he gets on a tear, he is an ugly customer." About noon one day, Hunt was in John Dipper's saloon on Merchant Street when he became involved in a quarrel with Dave Wilson and tried to shoot him. Bystanders intervened, but Hunt was too drunk to be stopped. He fought against those who prevented the shooting and was soon mixed up in a fight with a black man whom he tried to cut with a straight razor. The razor was knocked out of his hands, and he ran out of the saloon and down the street. As he ran, he pulled a revolver from his pocket and fired several shots into the air. Police Officer Horton heard the shots, pulled his own gun and started in pursuit. Officer John Williamson was on East Wood Street when he heard the shots and started toward Lincoln Square. He met up with Officer Horton, who was running across the square. They soon saw Hunt coming toward them, and they ordered him to drop his gun and put up his hands. He quickly surrendered. Hunt was arrested for assault and disorderly conduct. When asked why he had fired his gun in the street, he said that he was so drunk that he thought he was shooting at dogs.

In June 1895, a well-known whorehouse madam named Mattie Jones was arrested in her sporting house on Merchant Street. She was taken to jail and fined twenty-five dollars, which she promptly paid. However, Mattie was shocked when officers raided her house again the following day. This time, she was arrested, along with three of the girls who worked with her. She got a surprise when she went before Justice Peddecord and was fined fifty dollars, which was double the usual fine. She told the *Decatur Bulletin-Sentinel* that she believed the city was trying to put her out of business, which she couldn't understand since none of the other houses in the city were being bothered. Mattie couldn't pay her fine and was sent to the city jail. An hour later, one of her gentlemen friends appeared with the money, and she was released.

Mattie remained in business and was back in court, with a baby in her arms, on June 23, 1896. She was fined again for keeping a sporting house, and she promptly paid the fine. On a separate note, Mattie's baby died of cholera a little over a week later, on July 3. She was back in court again on July 27, this time charged with adultery. She pleaded guilty and paid a fine. In May 1897, Mattie's career as a Merchant Street madam came to an end. By this time, she was a physical wreck and was addicted to morphine, which she was taking on a daily basis. Homeless, she was taken to the country poor farm and died soon after.

A fight broke out in a Merchant Street saloon on June 21, 1895. The trouble was started by Mollie Cole, a well-known prostitute. It began when F.E. Brown, a cabdriver, came into Mackwell's Saloon with another prostitute, Lou Johnson. Mollie insulted the other woman, and Brown smacked her in the face. A man named Boyle took up the fight for Mollie, and a lively brawl was in progress when Officer Pete Dempsey appeared on the scene. He arrested Brown, but the other participants escaped.

In August 1905, Mrs. James Todd suffered a violent and unprovoked attack at the hands of her husband, a bartender at J.C. Bolay's tavern on Merchant Street. According to accounts, the Todds had been living separately for some time, and Todd had sued his wife for divorce, but she refused to sign the legal papers. On August 19, he had called her on the telephone and asked her to come to the saloon on the pretense of having something important to tell her. When she arrived, he took her into the back room and beat her mercilessly. Her screams drew tavern customers, who saw cuts on her face and marks and blood all over her dress. She returned home and called Dr. A.F. Withelroy, who treated her injuries. It took several stitches to close her gaping wounds. Her father, Augustus Verding, reported the beating to the police, but there were no laws regarding domestic violence at the time, and no charges were ever filed.

In February 1910, the police raided a soft drink parlor on Merchant Street for selling illegal alcohol. This was during the time of one of Decatur's liquor bans, and police officials stepped up raids in advance of the upcoming city elections to make it appear as though the law was being strictly enforced. A number of former taverns that had been converted into soft drink establishments were raided, and several were closed down once it was found that they had continued to sell liquor. On February 8, two police officers in plainclothes decided to investigate a parlor owned by Charles Wiefel on Merchant Street. The place turned out to be a "double-deck affair," as the newspapers called it, with a bar on the first floor and another in the basement. On the first floor was a long bar where the usual soft drinks were sold, but near the front of the bar was a sort of walk-in closet, the door to which was covered by a curtain. This concealed an entrance down to the basement. The door was kept locked, and no one was allowed to enter unless the employee working behind the counter unlocked it.

The two police officers, Park and Mays, walked in and stood outside the curtain. They told Cully Harriten, the counterman, that they wanted to go downstairs. Harriten didn't recognize them and unlocked the door. The officers went downstairs and found a room that was about twelve feet square, fitted with a small bar. About twenty men were crowded into the small space, and none of them paid any particular attention to the policemen. Park and Mays got the men talking and learned some of their names and even whether they were drinking beer or whiskey. A man named George Anderson was working behind the bar.

After observing the place for a few minutes (and likely having a drink or two themselves), the officers returned to the police station and swore out warrants. When they returned the second time, the subterranean bar was even more crowded than before. Charles Wiefel and Cully Harriten were arrested for keeping the place, and George Anderson was arrested for selling liquor. The patrons were turned out into the street, and the place was closed up.

The gambling raids of the late 1930s finally cleaned up Merchant Street for good. In the years that followed, legitimate businesses returned, and while a few taverns held out for a while, they were eventually pushed out by stores and restaurants. Today, Merchant Street is home to upscale eateries and boutique shops and is a far cry from the disreputable place it was at the turn of the past century. Most current residents have forgotten—or likely never knew—the history that rests in the stones and sidewalks of a place once regarded as one of the bloodiest in the city.

THE LEVEE

The most notorious vice district in Decatur's history was undoubtedly the Levee, a collection of businesses, hotels, saloons and gambling parlors that could be found next to the city's two train stations. The Levee extended from

The Levee District in the early 1900s.

Water Street on the west, running along Eldorado Street and the Wabash tracks, to the Illinois Central tracks on the east. The place became a magnet for criminals, drunks, gamblers, prostitutes and vice of every kind. Even in 1901, the newspapers stated that many people in Decatur would not go down to the Levee without a police escort—and even that would not guarantee their safety.

No one knows for sure how the Levee in Decatur got its name, but most likely it was a nickname based on several vice areas in St. Louis and Chicago. Both of these larger cities had districts dubbed the Levee, and the South Side Levee in Chicago was the largest in the country during the middle and late 1800s and into the 1900s. The district in Decatur seems to have gotten its start during the Civil War and may have been first named by the soldiers who passed through the city. Many of the soldiers had money to spend and, after arriving by train, went looking for drinks and female companions during the short time they were in Decatur. The taverns located near the train stations began to do an extraordinary amount of business (the Central Hotel was reportedly taking in over $100 an hour at its bar in 1863), and soon more taverns began to open nearby. The railroads brought thousands of people into the city, some of them for a short time, and the Levee offered an array of vice that was close at hand.

The lurid reputation of the Levee spread, much to the dismay of the legitimate businesses that operated there. There were a number of reputable hotels and restaurants that prospered in this part of the city, catering to railroad passengers and local residents who were not looking for illicit pursuits.

The most successful businesses were located just south of the Wabash station on a wedge-shaped lot that is cornered by both Front and Angle Streets. The first was a hotel called the National, which opened in 1886 and faced the Illinois Central Station to the east. To the rear of the hotel, facing the Wabash station, was a small restaurant that also served as a newsstand and sold drinks and tobacco to rail passengers. A small saloon was also connected to the hotel itself.

In 1906, a large portion of the triangular lot became the property of George W. Kraft, a businessman who owned the Whistle Bottling Works and three gold mines in Colorado and who also helped to start Decatur's first volunteer fire department. The National Hotel was torn down in 1907, and the Kraft Hotel was built in its place. Originally, Kraft had simply planned to add on to the National Hotel, but he abandoned the idea in favor of a new building. His business competed with another hotel, the Angle Hotel, which was built a few years before and opened at the south end of the triangle lot. The Kraft Hotel was one of the cleanest in the city. It had forty-eight rooms, each with a private bath and hot and cold running water. The main entrance faced toward the south end of the Illinois Central Station, and the place boasted a dining room and barbershop for travelers. In 1914, a new section was constructed, providing an additional fifty-one guest rooms. The expanded hotel also featured a large garage that today houses Decatur Auto Body. The garage still bears the original name on the outside and is the only part of the hotel still standing.

In 1953, the ownership of the hotel passed to Charles E. Witts, who would change the name to Hotel Charles and then to the Motor Hotel in 1960. Witts expanded the business to include a tavern, and it was later turned into the Flamingo Club, which offered food, drinks and live entertainment. The hotel closed for good in November 1966, but the building continued to be used for a number of years after that.

After the Flamingo Club closed, Stevie's Latin Village opened in the late 1950s and was later replaced by Dante's Italian Village, which is still remembered today for its pleasant atmosphere and fine food. Dante's closed down in the mid-1970s, and the building sat idle until 1987, when it was destroyed by fire. The site stands empty today, save for a few remnants of concrete and a lot of old memories.

Most memories of the Levee, however, have nothing to do with fine dining. Most of the stories and legends about the place concern the criminal activity that thrived there for so long. Incidents of drunkenness, robbery and violence became so bad on the Levee that the city police department opened a small auxiliary station and jail on Short Street in the early 1900s. This allowed officers and merchant policemen to lock up drunks and disorderly persons at the "holdover," as it was called, and then have them transported to the city jail the following morning. The Short Street station only contained two cells, but drunks were often just handcuffed to metal rings in the wall so that officers could drop them off for safekeeping and then go back to their beats. The Short Street holdover fell out of use by the 1930s and was closed down. The building was eventually demolished.

During its heyday, the Levee District made frequent copy for newspapers in town, all hoping to present some lurid or scandalous item. The incidents that follow are only a sampling of the stories that appeared during the liveliest years of the Levee.

In September 1885, the *Decatur Evening Bulletin* reported:

> *Late Saturday night, a portion of that distinct variety of society that inhabits the Levee district was holding high carnival in a room over Jimison's saloon on Morgan Street. Wine ran free and the merriment high, so high in fact that the police passing on the street below heard the sounds of revelry and saw a chance to make revenue for the city and raided the room. A part of the outfit put up bonds for their appearance and the others were locked up.*

In July 1895, a vicious brawl broke out in the saloon owned by John Doughtery on the Levee, leaving two men seriously injured. Two musicians, John Dressen and John King, were seated in the back of the tavern, providing music for the occupants with an old banjo and a fife. One of the customers, Frank Auburn, got tired of the racket the two men were making and went over to where King was seated and tried to take the fife away from him. Dressen protested, grabbed Auburn around the shoulders and roughly shoved him into a chair. Auburn jumped back up and went after Dressen, punching him in the left eye. The musician tumbled over a chair and fell to the floor, smacking his head. Dazed, he didn't see Auburn flee from the saloon.

John Doughtery began shouting at Dressen and King after Auburn left, berating them for causing trouble in his place. He grabbed hold of both men by the arms and started to drag them out of the tavern. King pulled away from him, and Doughtery turned and hit King in the chest, sending him sprawling over a stack of beer cases that were on the floor. King grabbed one of the bottles, and as soon as he got to his feet, he threw it at Doughtery, hitting him in the head. It struck Doughtery so hard that he was knocked unconscious. King jumped up and tried to kick the fallen man in the face, but Doughtery's son was nearby and managed to stop him.

Moments later, Officers Lord and Leech came through the front door and broke up the fight. King and Dressen were taken to the Short Street station, where they gave bonds for their appearance before Justice Peddecord. Dressen was sent to the hospital for treatment of his swollen eye, which doctors said he was liable to lose. He swore out a warrant for the arrest of Frank Auburn, but there was no record that it was ever served.

A bold, daylight robbery took place on the Levee in July 1895. At just after 8:00 a.m., a man came into High's Restaurant on Eldorado Street and asked High if he could make change for a dollar. High complied with his request, and after he had secured the change, the man went and stood in front of the building. A few moments later, a second man came around the corner and stood talking to the first man for a few minutes. The first man walked away, and the second man entered the restaurant. He sat down and ordered a sandwich and a cup of coffee. High took care of his order and then went into the kitchen for a fresh cup of coffee. When the owner returned, the stranger sipped the coffee and said that he didn't care for it. He paid for it anyway, along with the sandwich, and left the establishment.

A short time later, James Logan came in and ordered breakfast. When he paid for it, High put the money into his cash drawer and realized that it was empty—he had been robbed of more than twenty dollars. He realized that the last customer must have cleaned out the till when he went into the kitchen to get fresh coffee. High sent one of the kitchen boys to the police station, and he and Logan started in pursuit of the robbers. They reached the depot before any trains departed and notified the railroad patrolmen about the incident. No trace of the robbers was ever found.

In January 1896, Pat and Bill Morrison stumbled into a Decatur restaurant on the Levee. The two men had been drinking for most of the afternoon and were dangerously intoxicated when they entered the place. It was common knowledge that the owner, Charles Simmons, kept rooms in the back for prostitutes, and the Morrison brothers demanded to see one of the girls whom they had visited there before. Simmons replied that the girl was no longer there; she had moved to another establishment. Pat didn't believe the owner's story and told him very forcibly that if he was not allowed to see the woman, he would clean out the place. Simmons protested that the girl had left, but the Morrisons claimed he was lying, and one of them punched him in the neck. Bill Morrison grabbed a tin water pail and began to beat Simmons over the head with it, gashing open his forehead and drenching his shirt with blood. Witnesses later claimed that he would have killed the saloonkeeper if customers in the place hadn't stepped in and stopped the beating. The Morrisons fled but were arrested by Officer Leech (a name that appeared often in police reports from the Levee) after Simmons swore out warrants against them.

An actor named C.L. Luce was beaten and robbed on the Levee in February 1896. Luce, a former tailor shop clerk who resigned to join the Wild Goose Chase opera company, was assaulted by two men shortly after he disembarked from a Wabash train that arrived in town at 3:50 a.m. Luce started at once toward his home at 815 North Mercer Street but had only walked a few blocks before he was attacked by two thugs. He was beaten so severely with a club that he lost consciousness for almost a half hour. When he regained his senses, he found that his wallet, containing about fifteen dollars, and a pair of eyeglasses valued at ten dollars were missing. His head and face were badly bruised, scraped and bloodied, and his leg hurt so badly that he had difficulty walking. Too terrified to walk the dark city streets to his home, he returned to the railroad depot and waited until daylight before continuing his journey. On the way, he stopped at McKinness's drugstore at the corner of Monroe and King Streets and had his wounds dressed. He reported the incident to the police, but the assailants were never found.

Levee merchant policeman A. Ford had a close call one morning in April 1896. Ford was on duty about 3:00 a.m. and walked down an alley between Morgan and Broadway Streets, north of Eldorado. When he reached the north end of the alley at Cerro Gordo Street, he turned to walk back in the direction from which he had come. Ford was about halfway down the alleyway on his return trip when two men sprang from behind the stairway leading to the second floor of Bane's hardware store and opened fire on him with revolvers. Ford quickly pulled his own revolver and returned fire. A bullet grazed his arm, but he continued to fire. With bullets flying, the two men bolted out of the alley and into the street. They ran east on Eldorado to Morgan and then south on Morgan to North Street. At the corner of Morgan and North, Ford again attempted to shoot at the men, but his

Tramps and hoboes like these were commonly encountered on the Levee by Decatur's police officers. *Library of Congress.*

revolver misfired, and he gave up the chase. Officer Armstrong, who was working a few blocks east when he heard the shooting, arrived too late to stop the men from escaping. Ford's minor wound was treated after he filed a report. He had no clue as to the identity of the men who tried to kill him.

On July 13, 1896, Officer Leech broke the nose of a tramp who gave him trouble on the Levee. He had discovered a group of six or seven hoboes hanging around at the east end of the Wabash yards, drinking beer. When Leech approached them and told them to move on, one of the men, James Martin, refused. He insisted on going to the railroad depot instead. Leech struck the man lightly across the back and tried to steer him in the direction of the rest of the tramps, who were walking away. When he refused to leave, Leech hit him again, much harder, across the back of the head and knocked him to the ground. Martin protested the treatment that he was getting, and Officer Leech punched him in the face, breaking his nose. Officer Lord took him to the Short Street station, and he was later taken downtown in the patrol wagon. Martin, who claimed to be from Louisville, Kentucky, said that he was only trying to get a train ticket to Pana at the depot, but the officers wouldn't let him explain what he was doing. Leech dismissed his claims. He later found that Martin had left some cans of beer in the grass and didn't want to walk away without them.

Over the years, the Short Street police station on the Levee played host to scores of "guests," most of whom were too drunk to make it to a hotel. However, few of the guests were as distinguished as the one who slept in one of the station cells on December 19, 1896: John Hamilton, the Piatt County supervisor. Hamilton had arrived in the city by afternoon train and ended up in one of the saloons on the Levee. One drink led to another, and he went from tavern to tavern, boasting of his importance in Monticello and Piatt County. He continued to drink for as long as he could walk, which was until about midnight, and then he proceeded to pass out in a mud puddle on Front Street. He was discovered by Officer Holser about 1:00 a.m. Unaware of the identity of the drunk he found in the street, the policeman wrangled the man into a cell at the station and left him there to sleep it off. It was not until Hamilton was turned out the following morning that the officers learned his identity. He recalled nothing of the night before but knew that he had been robbed of about twenty dollars and his gold watch. Officer Lord escorted him to the train station and loaned him a hat to wear home. Hamilton begged the officers not to let the details of his embarrassing night become public, and Officer Lord might have agreed—but he never got his hat back. Irritated, he called the newspaper and reported the identity of the man who spent the night in the drunk tank.

August Gronkowski, crazed by drink, made two attempts to kill himself on the Levee in January 1901. He succeeded on the second try, swallowing a bottle of concentrated lye. Early in the evening on January 7, police officers received a call from a saloon on Cerro Gordo Street informing them that a man had shot himself. When they arrived, they found Gronkowski on his hands and knees in the middle of the floor, bleeding from a wound in his mouth. A revolver was lying next to him, and the police quickly took charge of it. A doctor was summoned, and he discovered that while the man had placed the revolver in his mouth and pulled the trigger, the bullet had bounced off the roof of his mouth and passed through his neck. It was a serious wound, the doctor said, but not a deadly one.

According to Mrs. Gronkowski, who spoke no English but communicated with the police through an interpreter, her husband was a terrible alcoholic and had tried before to kill himself while drunk. He was treated by the doctor and sent home. However, later that night, he drank a bottle of lye and died. It was later discovered that Gronkowski had been arrested the previous April on a charge of insanity. He was examined a few days after his arrest, and by then, the effects of the liquor he had been drinking had worn off, and he was released. His drinking on January 7, though, turned out to be fatal.

Three burglaries on the night of Sunday, January 17, 1904, angered Levee saloon owners. Three separate taverns, those of George Lancaster, M.C. Shiminski and Shurts & Shurts, were robbed during the early morning hours. Lancaster's saloon was entered through a window in a back closet, and the thieves made off with $19.00 from the till and four quart jugs of whiskey from behind the bar. The same robbers broke in the back door of the Shiminski tavern but only managed to get $1.50 in change, a few bottles of whiskey and a small keg of beer. Shiminski had taken his money home with him for the weekend. At the Shurts & Shurts saloon, the thieves made off with about $20.00 and more whiskey. They broke into the place by knocking out a pane of glass in a door that opened off an alley between the tavern and Kipp's grocery store. Robert Wilson, a clerk at the grocery store, was on his way home and heard the glass break. He looked into the front window of the saloon and saw a light burning and a man standing near the bar. Knowing that the tavern was closed on Sunday, he assumed that it was a cleaning man and that he had broken a bottle. He regretted later that he had simply turned and started on toward home.

The newspaper stated that Arthur Stubblebeam was "crazed by a thirst for blood" when he ran through the Levee on the night of September 7, 1905, frightening people and injuring Officer Ponewasch. The man began his night of terror on Railroad Avenue, not far from the Levee, when he broke into the home of the Carmen family and chased three children from the premises. After that, he attacked a man with a spade and was seen lurking around houses in the neighborhood. Charles Doolin and Frank Nanny, who lived nearby, saw Stubblebeam hiding behind a tree, and they notified the police. They followed him to the Levee, where they were joined in the pursuit by Officer Ponewasch. The policeman seized hold of Stubblebeam, but the man pulled a revolver and struck the officer in the head, giving him a painful scalp wound. He fled, but Ponewasch chased after him. As they ran, Stubblebeam turned and fired two shots at his pursuer. Both missed, and Ponewasch soon grabbed hold of the man again. He pulled his own gun and clubbed Stubblebeam with it several times, driving the man to the ground. He was dragged to police headquarters and locked up. Apparently, Stubblebeam had a reputation for manic and insane behavior but had never injured anyone before. He was sent to the insane asylum and died there two years later.

On the night of January 10, 1906, an African American porter named Samuel Ellis, who worked for a hotel on the Levee, caused quite a bit of excitement. Ellis had been a "dope fiend," taking morphine and cocaine for more than a year. He decided to clean himself up and purchased an over-the-counter elixir that was supposed to help him break the habit. Unfortunately, it didn't react well to alcohol, and one evening, after several glasses of whiskey, Ellis went on a rampage. Screaming with rage, he demanded that the hotel clerk give him money. When the man refused, Ellis threatened to take the money by force. He jumped over the hotel desk and picked the clerk up off his feet, holding him over his head. He threw the man down and then ran into a hallway, grabbed a chair and smashed it through a window. Still screaming, he went down the stairs to the basement and locked himself into the room where he lived. The police were summoned, and Officers Hendricks and Muthersbaugh arrived on the scene. They managed to break open the door and were confronted by Ellis, who claimed to have a knife under his bed that he was going to kill them with. The policemen overpowered the porter and secured him with handcuffs before searching for the knife, which they failed to find. Ellis was taken to jail, where he was examined by doctors, who stated that he had been poisoned by a mixture of the dope cure and whiskey.

A Springfield man was relieved of his money on the Levee on the morning of April 16, 1906. Edward Brockschmidt had arrived in Decatur by train and went to have some breakfast at a nearby restaurant. He had just finished eating when he was approached by a man who asked for assistance in getting some baggage from the express office of the Wabash station. He claimed to have three bags filled with jewelry, which he was taking to his home in Tolono and which had belonged to an uncle who had recently died. As the oldest son in the family, he said he had been placed in charge of the uncle's estate, but he did not have enough money to pay the transportation fees from the express office. There was a charge due of $31.50, and he did not have the cash. However, he did have a check for $335.00, payable to J.W. Woolford and signed by H.H. Blivens, from the First National Bank of Carbondale. The man claimed to be Woolford, and he offered to let Brockschmidt hold the check as security against a $31.50 loan. Brockschmidt, seeing no harm in helping the man, went to the express office. On the way, they met a man who claimed to be the express agent, and Brockschmidt paid him the $31.50

that was owed. Brockschmidt was then sent to the express office to await the delivery of the bags, which were in storage.

Brockschmidt waited for some time, and when the bags didn't appear, he began to get suspicious. After a while, he decided to telephone the First National Bank in Carbondale, and when he did, he was informed that they had never heard of H.H. Blivens, and he had no account with their bank. He next started looking for the express agent but was unable to find the man to whom he had paid the money. The agent on duty informed him that no one of that description worked in the office. He also learned that no bags were waiting to be picked up. He quickly realized that he had been duped out of the money. He wasted no time in informing the police of what had occurred, but by this time, it was too late to catch up with the two bunco artists.

Police raided the home of August Hackert, a coal miner who resided in the 700 block of East Eldorado Street, on January 4, 1910. Police Chief Bendure, Officers Welty, Park and Besslke and Wabash detective Dan Sullivan came to the Levee District residence in search of stolen property. The police had long suspected that the Hackerts were involved in a number of thefts that had occurred in Decatur, and they managed to get a search warrant for the family's home. In the attic, they tore up the floor and found four hundred or more shotgun shells, razor strops, safety razors, two dozen grain sacks, three bolts of silk and three or four bolts of muslin. The officers believed there was more to be found but decided to put the Hackerts under arrest before continuing the search. Chief Bendure and Officer Besslke waited at the coal mine later in the evening for August Hackert and his son, Walter. They were quickly put under arrest. The Hackerts had been under suspicion previously for boxcar robberies in the Wabash yards, but police had never been able to prove the case because the stolen goods were never found. It was believed this time that the family would "get a trip to the penitentiary," the newspapers said.

Although the Hackerts quickly posted bond, the search of their home continued. The police soon recovered everything from missing Wabash beef to imported soaps and an automobile cover. August Hackert tried to deny them entry back into the house, demanding to see a search warrant, but found that all was in order, and he had no choice but to allow the search to continue. Officers ransacked the house, tearing up floorboards on both the first and second floors and ripping apart the walls in the attic. Furniture was cut open and feathers removed from pillows. Even boxes of food were emptied to see if anything had been hidden inside. Such a quantity of missing loot from Wabash boxcars was recovered that Chief Bendure was forced to make an inventory list. The items on the list were the previously mentioned items, including four "Keen Kutter" safety razors and twenty packages of new blades, two boxes of .22-caliber revolver cartridges, five pairs of shoes, a side of smoked bacon, a new saw with the words "Wabash Railroad Co." engraved on it, one box of French toilet soap, twelve boxes of domestic soap, fifty boxes of "La Preferencia" cigars, paint brushes, bolts of lace curtains, wrenches, hammers and other assorted tools and more.

State's attorney John Hogan asked Mrs. Hackert about the razors. "Where did you get these, from Sears & Roebuck?"

"Oh yes, we got them from Sears & Roebuck," she replied in broken English.

"Just when did you get them?"

"I don't know," she answered. "I never shave."

The family all tried to account for where the strange assortment of items in the house came from but soon gave up. They could offer no explanation as to how, or when, the items were hidden under the floorboards of the house. "I know nothing, I know nothing," Mrs. Hackert told the police.

Federal officers raided the Levee in a search for opium in October 1914. Agents from the United States Secret Service, along with Decatur police officers, went to the Levee because of suspicions that opium was being distributed from at least two locations in the city. The first raid was carried out at a house on East William Street, but nothing was found. On the morning of Sunday, October 4, federal officers entered the old Beecher house at the corner of Cerro Gordo and Short Streets and took the place apart. Furniture and mattresses were cut open and searched. Carpets were taken up and cabinets were opened. The only questionable discovery was that of an old and broken opium outfit that did not look as though it had been smoked for some time.

Federal agents were searching for a Chinese immigrant, known only as "Charley man," who had worked as a cook in a number of Levee establishments. He had been arrested for throwing a meat cleaver at a man in a tavern at the corner of East Eldorado and Front Streets. He kept a room in the Beecher place, which is why the building had been searched, but no sign of him was found. Officers soon learned that word had leaked about the raid, and the suspect had left for St. Louis, where other agents continued the search. They had hoped to force him to reveal the identity of his drug source and the names of the men who were supplying opium in Decatur. No suspects were named by the federal agents, and while Decatur police officers were helping with the search, the secret service agents refused to offer any information—especially since it was likely a leak in the Decatur police department that had warned "Charley man" to leave town. The newspapers noted that there were a number of "dopes," or drug addicts, in the city and added that it was possible that a large distributing agency was operating in Decatur. There were no further reports about whether "Charley man" was ever caught, but opium raids continued in the city into the 1920s.

AFTER THE START OF PROHIBITION, many of the saloons on the Levee were converted into soft drink establishments, usually still selling liquor from back rooms or basements. Decatur's lackluster enforcement of the Prohibition laws became known all over the country, and the Levee remained one of the easiest places in the city to get a drink. The gambling parlors and the brothels continued to operate there throughout the next decade.

By the late 1930s, though, the Levee had changed. Many of the taverns and saloons had been pushed out, and while there were still plenty of places to get a drink, especially along East Eldorado Street, the Levee was a much quieter place. A newspaper interview with an Officer Adams noted that only a fraction of the arrests that once took place on the Levee were still occurring. He stated that only two men had been locked up at the Short Street holdover between June and January. Arrests for drunkenness and disorderly conduct had become a thing of the past. The newspaper writer added his own commentary on the demise of the Levee: "Such a tale of peace and quiet might well break the heart of a reporter. It makes him almost long for the good old days when men walked the Levee and drank and fought and now and then killed each other."

RED LIGHTS ON THE PRAIRIE

Prostitution in Decatur

Prostitution arrived in Decatur with the railroads. There may have been a few disorderly houses, as brothels were commonly referred to, in existence in Decatur prior to the late 1850s, but they didn't make news until after the start of the Civil War. Just as the Levee was created to serve the drinking and gambling needs of soldiers passing through the city, brothels also appeared to meet the demand. By the late 1800s, a segregated red-light district had been established in the 500 and 600 blocks of East William Street, and the sporting houses were mostly left alone to operate there. Occasionally, a raid would take place at one establishment or another—usually because protection payments had fallen behind—but most of those raids occurred outside the boundaries of the red-light district, which was a short two blocks away from the Levee.

The segregated red-light district was not the only place in the city where brothels could be found. Many of them, especially on the South Side of Decatur, catered to the workingmen of the coal mines, farmers, factory workers and traveling businessmen who avoided places like the Levee and other vice spots. Many of these brothels could be found on quiet residential streets and in downtown buildings, hidden carefully in plain sight.

Prostitution made good copy in the newspapers of the era, often shocking the more conservative residents of Decatur, who pretended not to know that the sex trade was operating in their midst. Some of the local prostitutes and madams—like a streetwalker named Sweet Sarah, whose exploits appeared almost weekly in Decatur newspapers during the early 1900s, and disorderly house owners like Red Ethel—became local characters.

On April 28, 1888, a young woman named Mollie Miller was arrested and confessed to keeping a house of ill repute on East Main Street in a home owned by Mrs. Elizabeth Davis. One newspaper editor commented:

> *The closing up of that den of temptation is* [the] *source of some great gratification to all decent people, especially those dwelling in that neighborhood and all who are compelled to pass by that house. There are several other dens in and out of the city that should also be closed up.*

Occasionally, neighbors of sporting houses complained to the police and managed to get them closed down. In February 1895, a woman named Katherine Hamilton swore out a warrant against the owner of a house down the street from where she lived. She went before the state's attorney and charged Eva Vahler with harboring an underage girl, Hettie Mercer, in a house of prostitution. Vahler was arrested, and Hettie, who had voluntarily gone to work as a prostitute, was returned to her parents.

In June 1895, Captain Holmes and Officers Bailey and Dempsey raided a bawdyhouse on South Main Street that was kept by a woman named Ruby Dawson. Four prostitutes were captured and taken to the city jail for the night. Police also raided a house on Merchant Street and arrested four more women. The keepers of the houses were fined twenty-five dollars each, and the prostitutes each had to surrender ten dollars.

"Last night, Captain Muthersbaugh and several officers made a hasty march on the Lou Johnson disreputable resort south of the city and captured several fallen angels," the newspapers reported in February 1896. A number of men who were "keeping company" with the ladies were also arrested, and the entire crowd was brought back to the police station and fined.

In the early 1900s, stories of white slavery were prominent in news reports and in lurid bestsellers that were penned by well-meaning reformers intent on doing away with prostitution and houses of ill repute. Many news stories cited cases of young women who were pressed into service as prostitutes and who did not willingly go to work in brothels. Once such case occurred in Decatur in February 1910, and the police learned of it after receiving a report about a drunken nude girl walking down North Water Street. The twenty-one-year-old girl's name was Viola Harris, and she was first seen at the Gushard store about 7:00 p.m. on Sunday, February 20. Followed by a number of jeering men, she stumbled into the store clad only in her chemise and stockings, apparently so intoxicated that she could barely stand. Shocked at the behavior of the people on the sidewalk, one of the store clerks opened an umbrella and shielded the girl from view until Officer Powell arrived. He took the girl to the Moran undertaking establishment, where she was given a blanket to cover herself. The crowd that had followed her was still milling about on the sidewalk when Viola was transported to police headquarters.

Viola had been staying in rooms rented by Peter Harris, above a tavern called the Bizzy Izzy on North Park Street. The second and third floors of the building were used as a house of ill repute. Viola was the sister of Mrs. W.W. Kish, who lived on South Colfax Street, and she told the police that Viola had been at a home for delinquent girls in Claremont, Indiana, since she was nine years old. She had moved to Decatur just three months before to live with her sister and brother-in-law and to work at a restaurant they owned. On Saturday night, Viola had telephoned to say that she would not be home that night, and before Mrs. Kish could reply, the receiver was hung up. Mrs. Kish made a search for her sister that night and on Sunday morning.

After the girl had been taken into police custody, Mrs. Kish and Officer Al Petty went to the brothel that was run by Peter Harris. Mrs. Kish told Harris that she knew the girl had been there and demanded the return of Viola's clothing. Harris at first denied any knowledge of Viola but later admitted that she had been there. However, he said that she had been drinking heavily and that any actions she engaged in were of her own volition. He surrendered the girl's dress, and Officer Petty placed him under arrest. After doctors examined Viola, they realized that the young woman had been drugged and given liquor and had been ill used by a large number of men who visited Harris's rooms. Mrs. Kish swore out a warrant against Harris for disorderly conduct, keeping a place for immoral purposes and enticing a woman into his place for immoral purposes. Harris paid a bond of $100 for his appearance in Judge Wadell's court the following Friday and was released. He quickly skipped town and was never captured.

Viola Harris took quite some time to recover from her ordeal. She remained unconscious for three days in the medical ward of the jail and eventually had to be placed in a straitjacket to prevent her from pulling out her own hair. When she finally awakened, she managed to drink a cup of water and told her sister that, to her knowledge, she had not been drinking on Saturday night. She said that she met Harris while working at the restaurant on South Park Street. Doctors believed that Harris gave her some sort of "knock-out drops" and managed to get her into the bordello. Viola slowly recovered from the terrifying experience and went on to lead a normal life.

Prostitution arrests and sporting house raids continued in the 1910s and 1920s, almost always avoiding the segregated area on East William Street. Raids that resulted in the arrests of dozens of people occurred, closing down bawdyhouses that managed to reopen again a few days later. Raids continued into the early 1930s, and more fines were given out, more houses were temporarily shuttered and more names printed in the newspapers, to the embarrassment of the men who frequented Decatur's brothels.

Despite attempts to clean up the city, the red-light district continued to thrive. It lasted until 1936, and when it was finally closed down, it was a major event. On the morning of March 14, newspapers reported the death of a local stockbroker named John King, who had been shot to death on the front porch of a brothel located at 545 East William Street, in the heart of the red-light district. The shooting, and the publicity that surrounded it, turned out to be the catalyst that closed down the segregated area for good.

The Tucker House brothel, located at 545 East William Street, the heart of Decatur's red-light district.

Kenneth Ogbin, a guest at the brothel and a former tavern owner and unsuccessful Republican candidate for Macon County sheriff in 1934, admitted to shooting King but claimed that it was an accident. Late on Saturday evening, Ogbin was sleeping and was awakened by the owner of the brothel, Alice Hutchings (aka Alice Tucker). She told him that two men were on the front porch shouting and pounding on the door, demanding to be let in. Ogbin took his .38-caliber revolver and went downstairs to tell the men they needed to leave. He opened the door, and King tried to push his way inside. Ogbin tried to push King back, shoving the barrel of his gun into the other man's abdomen. He then claimed that it accidentally went off. Ogbin fled from the house and, a few hours later, threw the gun into the lake. Later in the morning, he turned himself in when he heard that the police were looking for him. He had consulted with attorney L.E. Stephenson, who convinced him that this would be the right course of action.

John King, a forty-three-year-old stockbroker, was married and had a son in junior high school. King had offices in Decatur but had previously worked out of an office in the Wrigley Building in Chicago. In 1929, he lost most of his money in the stock market crash and moved to Decatur to work for Allen, Wiley & Jostes, an insurance and investment business. His father was Dr. John King, chief of staff of St. John's Hospital in Springfield. On the night he was shot, King and a drinking companion named L.A. Lynch had decided to end their night by paying a visit to one of the local whorehouses. They first went to a house operated by Della Smull, but when they were refused admittance, they went down the street to a house owned by Alice Tucker. Both men were very drunk, and they began to pound and kick the door when Tucker refused to let them inside. Tucker then stated that she went to an upstairs room where Ogbin was sleeping. It was believed that Ogbin was living in the house free of charge in exchange for working as Tucker's security man. Ogbin was well known in town. In addition to once running for the office of sheriff, he also once owned a tavern on East Eldorado Street. Alice Tucker had worked for him in his saloon before becoming the owner of the sporting house.

An ambulance was called to transport King to St. Mary's Hospital, where he was found to be in critical condition. Tucker was arrested, as were Betty Thompson and Joyce Cook, two prostitutes who worked for her. After Ogbin surrendered to the police, he was charged in the shooting and then charged with murder when King died from his wounds.

The shooting was followed by a series of raids on houses in the red-light district, on North Broadway and at the Central Hotel at 528 North Water Street. Police Chief H.J. Schepper and city attorney S. Everett Wilson

Above left: Kenneth Ogbin was arrested for King's assault and murder.

Above right: Alice Hutchings (aka Alice Tucker), keeper of the brothel where King was killed.

announced a deadline for all the brothels to be emptied by Monday morning. Any of the operators or prostitutes still on the premises, or even still in the city of Decatur, would be fined and arrested. According to newspaper reports, the brothels were abandoned by Sunday night.

Dozens of women, and embarrassed male clients, were arrested in the raids. The prostitutes were warned that should they be caught in Decatur again, they would be charged with vagrancy and sentenced to at least six months in jail.

The raids in the wake of the John King murder effectively ended the segregated red-light district in Decatur. Today, nothing of the district remains. All the houses that once stood on East William Street have been torn down and replaced by parking for newer buildings and empty, weed-infested lots. A period of Decatur's history has been completely erased and all but forgotten by those who vaguely remember the days when Decatur was still a wide-open town.

THE END OF THE CRIME ERA

My hands are clean and I am just as straight as the day I came into office.
—Chief of Police Joshua "Jack" Cooper

My administration has been clean, and I believe that Decatur is the cleanest city in the state.
—Mayor Harry Barber, just before his arraignment in circuit court

We will show that gambling and vice have not flourished any more in this administration than under any previous group of officials.
—Attorney W.J. Carey, in a rather unconvincing response to his client's claim that Decatur was the "cleanest city in the state"

If there were a single event that broke the hold crime had over the city of Decatur, it would have been the grand jury indictments of 1936. In March of that year, a grand jury was convened by special prosecutor Charles Evans to look into criminal activity in the city. Literally hundreds of witnesses were brought in from every walk of criminal life, and warrants were issued and arrests made on a daily basis. The probe focused mainly on prostitution, illegal liquor sales, gambling, racketeering and bribery of public officials.

Decatur newspapers began running small articles on the hearings, but soon the stories grew larger as editors began to slowly realize what effect they were going to have on the city. By late March, one newspaper referred to the hearings as "the most important investigation into gambling and vice in the county."

Near the end of the final scheduled week of hearings, ominous witnesses began to appear at the courthouse. A Decatur attorney named Everett Wilson was called in to answer questions about campaign expenditures from the 1935 elections. Wilson had been part of the election campaign of Decatur's mayor, Harry Barber.

A number of other witnesses, also called that same day, seemed unrelated to any political probe, but Prosecutor Evans was being careful not to tip his hand too early. He announced to the press, which had now taken a keen interest in the closed-door proceedings, that the witnesses he had called "may prompt the calling of additional witnesses and may possibly require the subpoena of some witnesses who had previously appeared."

The hearings took another turn the next day when a man named Hugh Davis was called to testify. Davis was the owner of the Stag Café and was a well-known political aide and friend of the mayor. Employees of the establishment were also called in, as was a man named Roy Hunter, who was at that time serving a prison sentence on gambling charges. Other witnesses included additional restaurant and tavern owners, all of them supporters of Mayor Harry Barber during the 1935 campaign.

Corrupt Decatur mayor Harry Barber.

The following day, the newspapers reported that the city was in a state of "grand jury jitters." With the actual proceedings being kept secret, the public could only infer what was going on from the identity of the witnesses who were being called. The newspapers were keeping a close eye on the lineup, especially after some witnesses were called who were connected to the mayor's campaign fund. By this time, there were few people in the city who were not anxious about the direction of the hearings.

More reports emerged, off the record, about the mayor's campaign fund. Barber reported that his account only totaled $747, all of which he had contributed himself, but testimony before the grand jury included at least one donation of $2,000—which had somehow disappeared. There was also a question about missing money that was supposed to have gone into relief funds to be used for meals for transients. This money, under the mayor's control, had also disappeared.

The witness list continued to grow. One witness was Ross H. Boyd, a city inspector of licenses who had the supervision of Decatur taverns and restaurants. Boyd was believed to be under investigation himself and hoped to postpone his own demise by appearing in front of the grand jury of his own volition. This was the case with many of the witnesses, many of whom had already accepted guilty charges in circuit court for vice violations. They had nothing to lose by testifying and much to gain if given shorter sentences or smaller fines.

The next day's testimony continued by recalling Roy Hunter, the former Decatur slot machine operator who was now in prison. Hunter's testimony was used to reinforce the word of Ross Boyd, and it spelled out a charge of political corruption on the part of the mayor for allowing gambling devices to exist in the city. The jury also recalled Stag Café owner Hugh Davis, who backed up a story told by Ross about the mayor allowing gambling devices and establishments to exist in Decatur in exchange for "donations" to his election campaign.

There were no witnesses called the following day, but Charles Evans told reporters that the jury was preparing indictments that would be signed by Judge C.Y. Miller, the official responsible for starting the initial investigation. Rumors were flying about who would actually be indicted. The list of names was long and included a number of city officials, some of whom were no longer in office.

Decatur waited impatiently for the final list, and it came two days later. Most of the names on the list were familiar ones, shaking the city to its core. Three of Decatur's highest officials were on the indictment list, and they were accused of crimes that ranged from conspiracy and bribery to gambling and prostitution. The three officials were Decatur mayor Harry S. Barber, Police Chief Jack Cooper and state's attorney Arthur Frazier.

The grand jury returned eight other indictments as well, naming seven tavern owners on charges of selling liquor to minors and one alleged gambler who operated a betting parlor. These indictments seemed to be almost an afterthought and were barely mentioned in the newspaper reports. The real show was the indictment of the city officials, which had Decatur in an uproar. All three of the men were served with arrest warrants, but Barber and Cooper quickly made bail after their arraignments. Frazier had left town during the grand jury hearings and claimed to be unable to return to Decatur because he was in the hospital in Chicago, recovering from a bout with the flu. He was arrested a short time later, but he also made bail.

There were three charges filed against Arthur Frazier: bribery, embezzlement and malfeasance. Most of the evidence against him came from Roy Hunter, the imprisoned slot machine operator. He testified that he had given Frazier a $1,000 bribe in return for being allowed to run slot machines in Decatur. The embezzlement charge concerned money that had been collected for fees but had mysteriously disappeared while in Frazier's possession. The malfeasance charge would be similar to the charges filed against Barber and Cooper—simply stating that he had violated his duties as an official by allowing gambling to be conducted in the city and doing nothing to curb it. This charge was solidified by the number of gambling parlor operators who testified against him, alleging first-hand knowledge by Frazier of their operations.

The only charge filed against Chief Cooper was that of malfeasance. Like Frazier, he had failed to do his duty as the head of law enforcement in Decatur, the grand jury said. According to testimony, he had known the names of the operators and the locations of both gambling parlors and whorehouses in the city and had allowed these illegal enterprises to continue. It was alleged that he even offered them protection, but no exchange of money or favors could be proven. Cooper attempted to defend himself in the press but only managed to give credence to the indictment. He first said that he "could see no possibility of an indictment against him, unless it was based on his failure to close the vice houses." He then went on to add that he believed the way that the whorehouses had been running was a practical plan. "The places have been operating for twenty-five years, and they cannot be stopped now," he said, endorsing the very illegal activities against which he had been charged with defending himself.

The greatest number of charges was filed against Mayor Harry Barber, who is still remembered today as the most corrupt city official in Decatur's history—or at least the most corrupt one who got caught. There were four indictments handed down by the jury against Barber. The first charge involved his false reporting of campaign expenditures, about which many witnesses testified, including campaign aides, friends and even gamblers and tavern owners who admitted "donating" money to the mayor's election fund. The amount was far more than Barber claimed he had received.

There were two charges against Barber for embezzlement. Before serving as city's mayor, Barber had been the supervisor for Decatur Township. Several witnesses, including friends and campaign supporters, testified that Barber had stolen relief money that had been intended for the poor and had converted it into private funds. The second charge (and the most ludicrous one) was also from the time when he was township supervisor. In this case, witnesses alleged that Barber had delivered township orders to Stage Café owner Hugh Davis in exchange for three turkeys, three potted plants and a diamond ring that was valued at sixty dollars. While this charge was not exactly the "crime of the century," it was another proverbial nail in the coffin of Barber's political career. There was no way he could continue to serve in an official capacity with four indictments against him, even if one of them was a little ridiculous.

The fourth charge, of general malfeasance, encompassed Barber's entire career as mayor of Decatur. It was stated that while in charge of the city, he had jurisdiction over the police department. While in this capacity, he had knowledge of the operation of gambling parlors and sporting houses in the city but failed to order the police chief to rid the city of these sources of illegal vice.

Barber stated in the press that he was sure that he would be cleared of any wrongdoing associated with the "false charges" brought against him. He sniffed at the rumors that had been floating around the city and simply stated that, because of the duties of his office, he had no time to dignify them with a response. He went on to claim that "disgruntled and disappointed politicians" had engineered the entire plot against him. The witnesses had been paid off and the grand jury was fixed, he claimed. All Barber wanted was a speedy trial so that he could prove that none of the charges was true.

As mentioned, all three indicted officials turned themselves in after the arrest warrants were issued, and all of them entered pleas of not guilty to the charges. Everyone was waiting to see what would happen next.

Days later, Chief Cooper became the first to fold. He resigned from his post as police chief, and prosecutor Charles Evans quickly dismissed the charges against him. He would never stand trial for the indictment that was handed down against him. Arthur Frazier soon followed Cooper's example, and the charges against him were also dismissed.

On March 2, 1936, Harry Barber turned in his resignation as Decatur's mayor. The charges against him were also dismissed. He refused to comment before the resignation letter was submitted, but when it was over, he announced that he would rest for a while before returning to his jewelry business. He was a weary and battered man as he posed for photographs and spoke to the press on the morning of his resignation. He claimed, as he would continue to do for years afterward, that he could have beaten the charges that had been brought against him.

Many people felt that justice had been served by filing charges against these officials and driving them out of office, but many more believed that the three had merely been scapegoats who had been offered up for sacrifice to appease the public. These same voices suggested that other public officials, and more powerful business leaders, had been just as involved in the gambling and vice operations in Decatur but that nothing would ever be done about it. How much of this was true? We may never know for sure, but it is interesting to remember that, despite serious charges filed against them, Barber, Cooper and Frazier were never punished, and all three men faded into relative obscurity.

DEATH BY ANOTHER'S HAND

A Collection of Decatur's Most Infamous Murders

Close to 100 murders have been committed in Decatur and Macon County since 1858, which is as far back as records obtainable go. That most of the persons charged with these crimes were found is shown by the fact that there have been many cases tried in the circuit court. However, in a number of cases, the name of the murderer was never known.
—Decatur Review, *August 3, 1924*

Perhaps because of its vice districts or the notoriety of being known as a wide-open place, the city of Decatur has been the scene of an inordinate number of murders since people started keeping records in the 1850s. Murders occur for a variety of reasons—sex, passion, greed, anger and liquor among them—and for the most part are easily solved. It was not uncommon for the police to be summoned to the scene of a murder in the Levee District to find the killer still standing over the body with a smoking gun in his hand. Other murders, while solved, stand out in Decatur's chronicle of crime as unique or unusual, and these killings deserve recognition, even more than a century later.

There have also been many murders in Decatur history that have remained unsolved. Previously mentioned deaths like those of Mike Vitale and Omer Davenport are among them. These murders have remained a puzzle throughout the years, the trail of the killers long grown cold. There is little chance that the killers of these men will ever be identified.

What follows is a collection of Decatur's oddest and most notorious murders, beginning in the 1890s and ending with a crime from the city's not-so-distant past. Not all of them were sensational, and many of them were never solved, but each of them stands out as worthy of mention in a record of how Decatur has earned its reputation as a dark and often bloody city.

The Lynching of Samuel Bush

In May 1893, a hanging that occurred in Decatur galvanized the black population of the city. This was not the public execution of a man who had been tried and convicted of murder in a court of law but a brutal lynching that city authorities tragically allowed to happen.

Lynchings were simply public murders by a mob. They were often racially motivated and were used as retribution for crimes alleged but not tried before a judge or jury. The victims were mostly always black, and the practice dates back to the turbulent days after the Civil War. In the Reconstruction-era South, members of night-riding groups, especially members of the Ku Klux Klan, carried out lynchings of African Americans.

Lynching with a racial tone was not limited to the South. The New York Draft Riots were sparked, in part, by competition for jobs between Irish-American immigrants and free blacks, and during the riots, eleven blacks were murdered, with many more beaten and their property destroyed. The riots led to a brief exodus of blacks from New York and helped establish Harlem as the center of black society in the city.

Around the turn of the last century, race riots broke out in cities all over Illinois, and many either started, or ended, with lynchings. In 1909, the city of Springfield was rocked with racial violence, leading to the death of many of the city's African American residents and also to the formation of the National Association for the Advancement of Colored People (NAACP). Another riot occurred in Cairo in 1909 with the lynching of a man named Will James. Postcards were printed of the lynching and mailed all over the United States. More riots, this time over labor disputes, occurred in East St. Louis in 1917, and two years later, riots also occurred in Chicago, causing an even higher death toll. Decatur was fortunate in that it was not the scene of a race riot, but what did occur in the city in 1893 remains a blight on Decatur's history.

On May 29, a woman who lived to the south of Decatur reported that a black man had assaulted her. This report was followed the next day by another alleged assault, this time involving a Mt. Zion woman. On June 2, Samuel Bush, who fit the general description given by the two women, was arrested near Sullivan and brought to the Macon County Jail in Decatur.

Anger simmered in the community and a few days later, about midnight, an armed mob appeared at the jail. According to accounts, several thousand people turned out, and the crowd included many women and children. Despite the lateness of the hour and a soaking rainstorm, the mob refused to leave. No efforts were made by the police to clear the streets or disperse the crowd. They stood, waiting for something to happen, for nearly two hours. At just after 2:00 a.m., a group of men, numbering about one hundred, marched on the jail from Wood Street. They were followed by about twenty riders on horseback. None of the men wore masks, but coat collars were turned up, long coats were worn and most of the men wore their hats pulled down low on their foreheads. Rain could be seen glistening off the barrels of shotguns and rifles and off the long blades of corn knives.

The group approached the jail and demanded that Samuel Bush be turned over to them. Deputy Sheriff Midkiff, who commanded a troop of special guards inside the jail, refused. The mob broke open the outer doors and pushed into the jail offices. Police Chief William Mason, who tried to reason with the men, was badly beaten, and the mob rushed at the jail door. The mob members had come prepared for the task, swinging sledgehammers and iron bars. When a hole had been punched through the concrete wall near the hinges of the iron gates, the door was removed, and the men pushed their way inside. The few guards who attempted to stop them were quickly subdued and the rest fled, leaving the mob to its purpose.

The first cell that the men reached was occupied by a black man named John Caldwell. He had convinced one of the guards to give him a candle so that he would not be mistaken for Samuel Bush in the darkness. One of the men took his candle from him and used it to light the way to Bush's cell. Using keys that had been taken from the guards, the cell was opened, and Bush was pulled out from under the cot where he was hiding. He was stark naked, weeping and shaking with fear. He was dragged out of the cell, protesting his innocence. The mob hauled him outside, and when they reached the street, cries began to erupt from the thousand or more people who were milling about. "Hang him!" they called. "Hang him!"

Bush continued to cry that he was innocent of the crimes he was accused of, but no one was listening. He was allowed to pray, and newspapers stated, "He began to sing and pray in plantation style." He was reported to have said that he hoped he would meet the people putting him to death in heaven.

During the late 1800s and early 1900s, lynchings were carried out all over America, especially in the South. The state of Illinois saw a number of these tragedies occur, including the murder of Samuel Bush in 1893. *Library of Congress.*

The mob members had failed to bring a rope with them, and since none could be found, they tied together horses' halters and fashioned them into a noose. The noose was thrown over a light pole at the northeast corner of Water and Wood Streets. A cabdriver was forced to bring his cab close to the pole, the doomed man was shoved atop it and the noose was roughly forced over his head. Bush's feet were left dangling in the air as the cab was driven out from underneath him. He slowly strangled, and witnesses later claimed that it took him nearly twelve minutes to die.

The mob gave three cheers for Decatur and for Mt. Zion, where many of the members of the party had come from, and then dispersed into the night. An hour or so later, Coroner Bendure received a telephone call informing him that a naked "Negro" was hanging from a light post downtown. The remains were retrieved and taken to Brintlinger's undertaking parlor. Once the body was taken down, pieces of the halters that had been fashioned into the hanging rope were obtained as gruesome souvenirs by people on the street. It was said that Brintlinger handed out pieces of the makeshift "rope" at his undertaker's parlor for several days afterward.

While many would later claim that the lynching was a spontaneous event, it was anything but that. The rumbles of the angry public had been building since the prisoner had been brought to Decatur by train a few days before. Curious crowds surrounded the train during its journey, and eighteen

Illinois governor Peter Altgeld was stunned by the news of the lynching in Decatur. He personally offered a reward for the arrest of the perpetrators, but it was never collected. *Illinois State Historical Society*.

men had actually tried to stop it near Bement, but they arrived too late. Several hundred onlookers met the train when it arrived in Decatur, and they followed Bush as he was brought to the jail. Decatur's police chief had been given responsibility for the prisoner since the Macon County sheriff, Peter Perl, decided that the arrival of Samuel Bush would be the perfect time to visit the World's Columbian Exposition being held in Chicago. He preferred the wonders of the World's Fair over the political millstone of a vigilante lynch mob. When he returned to Decatur, he admitted that he had read about the lynching in the Chicago newspapers but didn't see the point in returning home and cutting his vacation short since the excitement was already over. Many in Decatur shared his opinion. There were few who seemed to regret the tragedy, as evidenced by the fact that a grand jury failed to indict anyone for Bush's murder.

Illinois governor Peter Altgeld was stunned by the incident and called the lynching "a diabolical murder and an outrage to the state." He offered a reward of $200 for the arrest of anyone involved in the crime, but no one was ever charged, and not a single dollar of the reward was ever collected.

The lynching of Samuel Bush was largely dismissed as a minor incident of violence at a time when blacks were considered second-class citizens at best. The event has never been commemorated and is mostly forgotten in Decatur today.

THE COLDBLOODED MURDER OF LOUIS WILSON

The city of Decatur was shocked in January 1895 when an eighteen-year-old man named Louis Wilson was gunned down at a dance by a rival named George Tucker. The two men had argued about the affections of a young woman, but what should have been nothing more than a heated disagreement turned into a murder.

The Wilson brothers, Ed, Marvin and Louis, lived in a small house on West Eldorado Street, near the fairgrounds and just west of the Wabash Railroad. A young Springfield woman named Clara Morthland had been a guest at her sister's house, and she became acquainted with Louis Wilson and George Tucker, both of whom lived nearby. Both young men had apparently fallen for her. On the night of January 12, the Wilsons held a dance in their barn, and Clara came in the company of Louis Wilson. However, her later testimony stated that she told him that if Tucker came, she was going to go home with him. Wilson was allegedly satisfied with this and escorted the pretty young woman to the dance. Tucker arrived at the dance later in the evening, and there was no ill will between the two young men—at least until the liquor started to flow.

About 11:00 p.m., Tucker prepared to accompany Clara home. As he left the dance, Louis and Marvin Wilson followed him out into the yard. According to one version of events, a few words were exchanged, and Wilson and Tucker came to blows. In the midst of the fray, a pistol shot rang out, and Louis sank to the ground with a loud groan. Realizing what he had done, Tucker jumped over a fence and ran down the road.

Meanwhile, Wilson lay twitching and bleeding on the ground. Startled guests emerged from the dance at the sound of the shot and found Marvin cradling the body of his brother in his arms. Blood was pouring from a wound near his left eye, where the bullet had entered. Ed Wilson quickly arrived on the scene. He had been playing his fiddle at the dance, and when he saw Tucker and Miss Morthland leave, followed by his two brothers, he hurried after them because he was afraid there would be trouble. Ed helped his brother carry Louis into the house, where he was placed on a makeshift bed near the stove.

Clara Morthland's brother, Cicero, was coming up the railroad tracks to the dance and was about one hundred yards away when he saw the flash of a revolver and then saw Tucker run south on Oakland Avenue. When Morthland reached the house and learned what had happened, he got a horse and rode quickly to the house of Dr. Bain Walston. The doctor found that the bullet had entered at the corner of Wilson's left eye, passed behind the right eye, severing the nerve, and lodged in his brain. There was no hope for the young man, he said.

Cicero Morthland and Ed Wilson went downtown and notified the police of the shooting. Officers Baylor, Cross and Muthersbaugh went to Tucker's home and arrested him at 2:00 a.m. He offered no resistance, and he was locked up in the county jail. He said that he had thrown the revolver away near Oakland Park. He first told the police that the Wilson brothers had jumped him and that the shot had been fired by accident, although he later changed his story to say that Louis never actually hit him and that he had been standing several feet away when Tucker fired the shot. He did swear that the Wilson brothers threatened him, and he had drawn the gun to try and get them to back off.

Police officers were quick to dismiss his excuses. Tucker had been arrested a few times before for disorderly conduct and displayed considerable nerve when talking about the matter. Officers later reported that he did not seem to be in the least concerned about Wilson's condition or whether he lived or died. He was also foolish enough to say that he planned to make things "hot" for the other Wilson brothers when he got out of jail. The police discovered that they were justified in their disbelief in Tucker's story after they interviewed witnesses at the dance.

Marvin Wilson's story was especially damning to Tucker. He told the police:

> *I was at the southeast corner of the house when Tucker and Miss Morthland came out. None of us wanted him to take the girl home because we did not think he was the proper person to keep her company. I went out there to protect Louis, if I could, and had only been there a few seconds when the couple came out. Louis came out almost immediately after. Tucker and the girl had almost reached the corner of the house and were only a few feet from me. My brother was several feet behind them. There was not a word spoken. The first thing that I knew, Tucker wheeled around and, drawing his revolver, fired at Louis. I saw him fall, and then Tucker ran up to me and said "stand back." I did and he ran southwesterly, to the corner of the lot, jumped into the road and disappeared.*

It was later learned that the Wilson brothers had made some threats toward Tucker and that he had come to the dance that night expecting trouble. Louis had apparently made some sort of comment about thrashing Tucker during the dance—a comment that was repeated by Clara Morthland as she and Tucker were leaving. She believed that this might have been what set the man on edge and that he had shot Louis because he feared being attacked.

Ed Wilson didn't believe that Tucker felt threatened. He believed that he had come to the dance looking for trouble, not fearing it. Ed was not aware of the disagreement between Tucker and his brother, but he had known Tucker for about two years and never liked him. He was surprised to see him at the dance and believed that he had been drinking before he arrived there because he was in such a bad humor. He recalled the incidents surrounding the shooting:

> *Tucker started away from the barn by himself and Miss Morthland followed him. I was playing for the dance and when they went out, I went to the door. My brothers went out just ahead of me. I knew how Tucker had been all night and I thought there would be trouble. Just as I got to the door, a shot was fired. Tucker was then about ten feet ahead of Miss*

> *Morthland. My brother was about two feet from Tucker and I did not see any scuffle but heard Tucker say "Stand back, damn you, or I'll shoot." Then, he shot right away. My brother fell and Tucker started to run. My other brother was standing near and Tucker said to him, "Stand back, you son of a bitch, or I'll shoot you, too!" Then, he ran away. My brother had no weapons.*

At just after 8:00 a.m. on the morning after the dance, Louis Wilson died of his wounds.

The charges against George Tucker were changed to murder, and he remained in jail until he went on trial in March. The prosecution quickly presented its case and left the jury to deliberate. The case seemed a simple one, made even simpler when it was learned that Tucker had borrowed the revolver from another man before going to the dance that night. The prosecution stressed to the jury that this proved Tucker had gone there with the intention of causing trouble. The jury returned on April 1 and found Tucker guilty of manslaughter. It sentenced him to one year in the penitentiary. The jurors refused to talk about the case, but it was learned that Tucker's guilt was quickly decided. However, numerous ballots were taken concerning his punishment before a final verdict was reached.

Murder in the Levee District

The most sensational murder to occur in Decatur in the early 1900s was the brutal slaying of Joe Ricketts, an employee of the Pacific Express Company and a well-known young man in town. Ricketts was beaten to death almost within the glare of lights of the Wabash station, and after more than a century, his murder remains unsolved.

Ricketts was only twenty-one years old when he was killed outside his place of work on Monday, August 28, 1905. His death was a mysterious one, and newspapers at the time called it "the most foul and cold-blooded murder that has ever occurred in Decatur." The biggest mystery in the whole affair was that there seemed to be no reason why anyone would want to kill Joe Ricketts.

Joe was born and raised in Decatur, the son of J.H. Ricketts, a respected carpenter. As a young boy, he went to work for Ehrhart's grocery store at the corner of Green and Union Streets and soon became a familiar face to everyone in the neighborhood. He began work there delivering goods

Joe Ricketts worked at the freight office of the Wabash Station on the Levee. He was killed only steps away from where he worked, and yet his murder was never solved.

to nearby customers with a basket and a little wagon. As he got older, his responsibilities increased, and he became the head deliveryman for the grocer. His duties took him to all parts of the city, and he became known to hundreds of families throughout Decatur. He was a beloved character, known for his good nature, pleasant smile and cheerfulness. He went above and beyond what was required of him for his job, and people remembered him for it. After working for Ehrhart's for several years, he worked for the Conrad Grocery until it closed and then worked for a time for his father in his construction business. In July 1905, Ricketts took a position working nights for the Pacific Express Company at the Wabash station. Joe stayed the entire night at the station, taking care of the express office during the early morning hours. He reportedly enjoyed the job very much, and his supervisor, Pete Roby, had nothing but good things to say about him.

The admiration that everyone seemed to have for Joe Ricketts was what made his death so puzzling. Joe was killed at the northwest corner of the Ward commission house, a building adjoining the Pacific Express Company on the West Side. His body was discovered by W.A. Owens, who was walking between some freight cars and the commission house about 9:30 p.m. He called to two men who were working in the Wabash yards, and they approached the body with a lantern, fearing that someone had been hurt. When they realized the man was dead, they gave the alarm to the stationmaster, who notified the police. When police officers arrived, they realized the dead man was Joe Ricketts.

Ricketts's body was lying in a pool of blood, just a few feet away from the railroad tracks. Two clubs, both bloody at one end, were found near the body, and it was plain that the young man's head had been pounded with several solid blows. There was no evidence of a struggle, and it did not appear that he had been robbed. When officers examined his body, they found that his skull had been crushed, splintering the bone and exposing the brain beneath. His forehead had been smashed in, covering his face and clothing with blood. His hands were stretched out straight, and he was flat on his back. As he fell, his heels had dug up a little place on the ground, and it looked as though the first blow that struck him had knocked him down where he stood. Joe's cap was lying about two feet away from his body. There was nothing about his hands to suggest that he ever got a chance to defend himself.

Joe had been missing for about an hour and a half. Peter Roby had first gone looking for him about 8:00 p.m., shortly after he was seen talking to a customer, A.L. Onstott, in the south door of the express office. Joe had been laughing and cheerfully performing his duties at the time, but he went to his death just a short time later, within easy shouting distance of his friends and co-workers and scores of passengers who came and went on the trains throughout the evening.

Lights were used to illuminate the dark and isolated area where Joe's body was found. At first, it seemed strange that a man whose duties were in the express office should have been at such a spot. The commission house was a large brick building that faced toward Cerro Gordo Street. It was next to the express office, but Ricketts's body was found on the far side of it. Peter Roby had an explanation, however. He said that since there was no bathroom in the express office, he and Joe often ducked outside at night and releived themselves in the dark corner. He believed that Ricketts must have been surprised either while on his way to the secluded area or as he was leaving it. Deputy Sheriff Hendricks had another idea. He thought that Joe might have come across thieves who were pilfering melons from a nearby freight car, and when he startled them, they beat him to keep him quiet.

As word began to spread about the murder—and the popular victim—a large crowd hurried to the scene, making it difficult for the police officers to search for clues. The body was left in place until word was sent to the coroner, but Dr. Buxton was out of the city, forcing Justice Keeler to come and act as coroner. The body was eventually taken to Hawkins & Davis's undertaking parlor, where an inquest was held the following afternoon.

In the meantime, at the Wabash station, the police continued their search of the grounds. Several dependable men from the crowd were recruited to assist them in their efforts. When nothing besides the two bloody clubs was found, officers began scouring the city for anyone who had information about the murder. Messages were sent to surrounding cities, ordering that any strangers be taken into custody and held for questioning. By 2:00 a.m., eight men had been arrested in Decatur and another man had been taken into custody in Taylorville. All of the men were eventually released since no evidence could be found against any of them.

On August 29, the mysterious murder became even more puzzling. A witness had come forward to say that he had seen three people in the vicinity of the spot where Ricketts's body had been found, likely within ten minutes of the murder. Marlon Spencer, a laborer who had lived in Decatur his entire life, had been on his way to his brother-in-law's house at about 9:00 p.m. on the night of the murder. Spencer lived on Wabash Avenue and left his house, walking east until he came to Morgan Street. He turned south along the railroad and, at the crossing, cut across to head toward the depot. Spencer was about halfway across the yards when he was attracted by the sound of a man clearing his throat. He turned his head and saw a man standing against the signal house at the southwest corner of the crossing.

There was a bright light at the crossing, and Spencer said that he would have no trouble recognizing the man if he ever saw him again. The man was leaning against the signal house and was dressed in a dark suit and a black, soft hat. He was slim and had a light-colored, heavy mustache. The man was holding what Spencer thought was a shovel. He later realized that it could have been a club or a stick. The man was not looking in his direction. Instead, he was staring rather intently toward the east.

Spencer was walking in the direction that the man was looking but did not believe the man saw him there because he was focused so intently on something in the distance. At this point, a line of boxcars prevented Spencer from seeing the commission house, but as he got closer, he heard the distinct voice of a woman speak from the shadows. "I'm going this way," she said. Spencer looked up and saw a woman walking with another person in the darkness. He could not tell if the woman's companion was a man or another woman, nor could he describe the woman, other than to say that she was wearing some kind of dark-colored dress.

Spencer thought nothing of the incident at the time, and he never saw Ricketts's body, which was probably already lying in a bloody patch next to the commission house. He walked on to the station and went inside. When he did, he looked at the clock and noted that it was 9:10 p.m. He only remembered the time because it was getting late and he was expected at his brother-in-law's house. Spencer went home by another route, and because of that, he knew nothing about the murder until the following day. Realizing that he might have a clue for the police, he went downtown and reported what he had seen. Sadly, the information led nowhere, and if the man, the woman and her unknown companion had any connection to the murder, they were never found.

Joe Ricketts was buried on August 30 in Greenwood Cemetery. His funeral was the largest ever held at the First Christian Church and was filled with Pacific Express Company employees, railroad men and scores of people who knew and loved Joe from his days of service as a grocery deliveryman.

By early September, the case was already growing cold. The police had been over every clue several times and had questioned hundreds of people about the case. They were nearly overcome with theories and ideas from well-meaning citizens, but none of them led to the killers. Officers diligently followed up on everything that came along, but as more days passed, it became less likely that anything useful would be found. In time, investigators moved on to other cases, and Joe Ricketts's murder became less and less of a priority.

As with every unsolved case, it remains open today, but it's unlikely that any new information will ever emerge about a murder that's now more than a century old. It seems almost certain that the identity of Joe Ricketts's killers will forever remain a mystery.

The Unsolved Murder of Wilbur Stephenson

Another of Decatur's most puzzling unsolved murders was that of Wilbur Stephenson in February 1917. The hardworking young man was shot to death by a burglar who tried to break into the garage of Stephenson's employer, H.I. Baldwin. Wilbur had worked as a chauffeur for the Baldwins for some time, and one winter's night while they were out of town, he interrupted a thief at his work and paid a fatal price for it.

Wilbur Stephenson was a well-liked man around town, but he had had an unusual life, to say the least. Wilbur's mother had been a teenager in Monticello, Illinois, when she met his father, James Stephenson, an attractive stranger who came to Monticello on business. The two fell in love and, after a hasty marriage, went to North Dakota, where Stephenson had business interests. Wilbur was born a few years later, but his mother died when he was only fourteen days old. When she was brought back to Monticello for burial, Stephenson took Wilbur to his grandparents, Mr. and Mrs. John Miller, who lived in Decatur on North Water Street. He asked them to care for the boy temporarily and then promptly disappeared.

When Wilbur was two years old, his grandmother died, and his grandfather, a fine old man who was a beloved figure in the neighborhood, became the boy's only family. Wilbur thrived in his grandfather's care. The two went everywhere together, and it became a common sight to see the little boy holding onto Mr. Miller's hand as they walked down the street or ate dinner at a local restaurant. When Wilbur was five, John Miller, a bachelor uncle and Decatur policeman, moved into the house and began helping to take care of the boy. Sadly, the elder Miller died later that same year, breaking little Wilbur's heart. For many weeks, he refused to be comforted, crying for the man who had been his caretaker, teacher and best pal. Uncle John jumped at once into the role of parent for the boy, and as his sadness passed, Wilbur came to love John as much as he had loved his grandfather.

During all this time, nothing more had been heard from the boy's father. Then, one spring day when Wilbur was playing with several other children on Marietta Street, a strange man stepped from the sidewalk and snatched him up. The boy yelled and kicked, but the man ignored him. He simply held him tighter and started off down the street. The kidnapper turned out to be the boy's long-lost father, who was alleged to have heard that John Miller was dead and that part of his estate, a sum of $3,000, now belonged to his son.

Fate intervened in the life of Wilbur Stephenson. As his father carried him down the street, an automobile pulled up next to the man and the struggling child. The driver of the car was Don Lehman, the son of Decatur's sheriff, George Lehman. He asked the man if everything was all right, and Stephenson replied that his son was very sick—would it be possible for him to drive them to the Angle Hotel, near the Wabash station? Lehman agreed and dropped them off at the hotel a short time later. He thought no more of the incident until he arrived at the courthouse and was greeted with the news that children on Marietta Street had reported the kidnapping of Officer

John Miller's nephew. He told the police of his passenger and the trip to the hotel, and officers wasted no time in capturing the father. Judge Cochran was happy to give official custody of the child to John Miller.

Stephenson was released with no charges filed against him. It was a confusing case, and since he was technically still the legal guardian of Wilbur at the time he took him, he could not be charged with kidnapping. He permanently lost custody of Wilbur, however, and moved to New Mexico. He was not heard from again until Wilbur turned twenty-one, when he wrote to his son and asked him to come to New Mexico and live with him. Wilbur replied that he would come for a visit but that his home was in Decatur. Unfortunately, he was never able to make the trip—he was dead just one year later.

Wilbur's uncle died when the boy was just sixteen, and he went to live with another aunt and uncle, Mr. and Mrs. J.E. Miller, who lived on North Church Street. He had grown to be a likable young man with many friends, and he worked hard during his years at Decatur High School. After he graduated, his interest turned to mechanics, and he started working with automobiles. He worked with several dealers and then went to work as a driver for the H.I. Baldwin family, taking care of several automobiles they owned and driving the family around town. He was happy with his new position and was given a room in the staff area of their home. He was a valuable employee—and friend—of the Baldwins and was very well paid.

By February 1917, Wilbur had worked for the Baldwins for just over two years. Around the middle of the month, the family took a trip to Louisville, Kentucky, and left Wilbur in charge of things at their home at 452 West Main Street. On Thursday night, February 22, Wilbur invited two friends, Sidney Moeller and Carroll Belden, to stay the night with him. For a few nights, he had seen a man prowling around the garage in the darkness. He feared that the prowler intended to steal an automobile from the garage or break into the house. He wanted his friends along for support, and late on Thursday evening, they decided to lie in wait and see if the man came back. They stationed themselves in the summer kitchen, with a clear view of the garage, and kept their eyes peeled for any sign of movement. Just after 1:00 a.m., they heard the alley gate open and saw the dark shape of a large, broad-shouldered man head into the garage.

Wilbur sprang to the door and threw it open and at the same time shouted at the man to throw up his hands. The young man had a revolver firmly clenched in his fist, but before he could even raise it, the man in the darkness fired his own gun. The retort of the pistol was deafening in the confines of the garage, and Wilbur reeled backwards when the bullet struck him. He would have fallen if Moeller and Belden had not reached for him as he spun backwards. The intruder rushed past them and vanished into the night. The boys had little time to worry about it. They had their hands full carrying their friend into the Baldwin house. Wilbur was bleeding badly from a wound in his neck and had lost consciousness. One of them called the police and a doctor, and Moran's ambulance was sent to take Stephenson to the Macon County Hospital.

When the police arrived at the house, Moeller pointed out the direction in which the intruder had run. Bloodhounds were used to follow his trail, running east along West Main Street to Lincoln Square and, from there, south to the Myers Hotel. The police rushed to the room of a young farmer who had just registered, but the startled man did not match the description of the burglar and could verify his whereabouts during the hours before. The trails of the farmer and the burglar had apparently crossed and the dogs had become confused, leading the officers to the hotel.

The killer's trail went cold.

Wilbur Stephenson had been rushed to the hospital and was immediately taken into an operating room. Doctors worked frantically but were unable to find the bullet that had struck him in the neck. Even after using an X-ray machine, the bullet eluded them. It was finally discovered embedded in his neck at the base of his skull behind the right ear. It was removed, but by then it was too late, and Wilbur died on Saturday at 3:15 a.m. He never regained consciousness.

The police worked diligently on Wilbur Stephenson's case for months, looking for his killer and seeking answers to some lingering questions, such as how Wilbur could have been shot in the back of the neck if he and the intruder were facing each other when the fatal shot was fired. After Wilbur was shot, Moeller and Belden said that the man ran east across the backyard, crawled through a hole in the fence and disappeared. The police wondered why he simply didn't go back through the alley gate. It was dark in the yard, and the police had to use flashlights to find the hole in the fence, so how did the killer find it so easily?

Suspicion was cast on Wilbur's friends for a time, but no one could think of any reason why they would have wanted the young man dead. The investigation seemed to point to the idea that Wilbur Stephenson didn't have an enemy in the world. This left only the idea that he had been killed in the commission of a robbery by a burglar who was never found.

Decatur's First Murderess

The first woman ever convicted of murder in Decatur was Josephine Cooper, who was forty-five years old in 1921, the year of her arrest. According to accounts, a man named James Parker had moved into the Cooper home at 505 East King Street in 1920. At the time, he was renting a room from Josephine, but the two soon became lovers. It was widely announced that they planned to be married, but something soured those plans. It is believed that Josephine fell in love with someone else, a man named J.W. Gordon, and that she found Parker to be a little harder to get rid of than she had first thought.

Parker eventually made the fatal mistake of signing over a $1,000 life insurance policy to Josephine, and that was apparently the motive she needed to commit murder. Several letters were later discovered that she had written to her other lover, Gordon, asking him to supply her with poison. While it was never proved that Gordon actually got it for her, she apparently obtained it from somewhere.

James Parker soon became seriously ill. He deteriorated quickly and died just two days after showing signs of some mysterious ailment. His body was discovered in the Cooper home, and the police immediately suspected foul play. Josephine was a very clumsy killer, as Parker's became the fourth body to be found in her home in just a few years.

The first had been that of Charles Blake, another boarder, who had died in 1913. Josephine's husband, Oliver Cooper, had died mysteriously in 1917, and three years later, her uncle, Albert McDaniel, died suddenly as well. After Parker's body was discovered, the coroner refused to sign a death certificate until a formal inquest could be held. A preliminary report from the unlucky man's autopsy showed that his internal organs contained arsenic in lethal quantities.

J.W. Gordon became the leading suspect in Parker's murder, and the police quickly placed him under arrest. Under questioning, he admitted that he had received letters from Cooper asking for poison, but he denied giving it to her. He also confessed that he had been a rival with Parker for the woman's affections but that he had never harmed the other man. He believed that it was Cooper who had killed him—and detectives agreed. Gordon was later set free due to lack of any evidence against him.

Cooper was arrested and put on trial in March 1921, and the testimony that was heard in the courtroom proved to be a strange and often convoluted tale of murder, insanity and horror.

State's attorney C.F. Evans made the opening statements in the case, outlining the events as they had occurred. He told the courtroom that in 1920, Josephine Cooper was operating a boardinghouse in her home on East King Street. James Parker was a boarder there, and the two became lovers, up until the time Gordon entered her life. According to later testimony from Jennie Godwin, who did Cooper's washing, Cooper and Gordon went to Chicago for a few days in early 1921 and stayed at the Fort Dearborn Hotel as husband and wife. Jennie had received a postcard from Cooper while they were away. The two remained lovers beyond the time of Parker's death, and although Gordon was married and living with his wife, he often posed as a widower and told people that the woman he lived with was his stepmother.

During the time that Parker was living with Cooper, Gordon joined the Supreme Tribe of Ben-Hur, a national fraternal organization that later became Ben-Hur Life Insurance. He took out an insurance policy; he told the examining physician that he was a widower and had the policy made out to his brother. Josephine Cooper joined the same lodge, and then, later on, Parker joined as well. He had his policy made payable to Cooper, and initially her policy was payable to Parker. She later changed it so that, in the event of her death, Gordon would collect instead. She never made Parker aware of the change.

As Cooper tired of Parker's affections, the state's attorney revealed that she made other attempts to get rid of him. She often told friends and neighbors that he was cruel to her and beat her. She tried to concoct a plan with a part-time boarder, Haven Whitehouse, to have a fake telegram sent from Parker's mother in Oklahoma, asking him to come home. Whitehouse declined to be involved, and when she asked Cooper why she wanted to make Parker leave, she was told that Gordon treated her right and she liked him better.

Another witness who took the stand against Josephine was Amanda Ely, who lived across the street from the boardinghouse. She stated that she had seen Gordon at Cooper's house many times and that she was also a witness when Cooper asked Haven Whitehouse about sending the false telegram. This event occurred about one week before James Parker became ill. A few days later, Cooper was complaining to her neighbor and told her that she wanted to quit keeping a boardinghouse and go back to work, but Parker wouldn't let her. But, she added, "I and a friend of mine have a plan to get rid of Parker." Three or four days later, Parker became so sick that he was unable to get out of bed.

About this same time, Cooper wrote several letters to Gordon, who was working in Blue Mound, and asked him for "something to put in Parker's coffee." She also wrote that she wanted Parker to die away from home so that no one would suspect that she had anything to do with his death. Although Cooper didn't know it, her lover was hardly faithful to her. In fact, he was also keeping company with a Blue Mound woman named Addie Farrow, who believed that he was a widower. Gordon actually showed one of Cooper's letters to her, and after learning of Parker's death, it was Farrow who went to the police with her suspicions.

When Gordon was arrested, he first denied receiving the letters but then took police officers to his garage, where he had hidden them, and turned them over. However, he was adamant about the fact that he had not given Cooper the poison that she asked for. Eventually, investigators came to believe him.

The prosecution maintained that after Parker became sick, Dr. W.A. Dixon was called and suggested that Parker be taken to a hospital, but Cooper objected. He also said that, following Parker's death, she had not only collected on his life insurance policy but also managed to get the pay that was due to him from the Wabash Railroad, where he worked. When arrested, she was in possession of Parker's watch and fifty-eight dollars in cash, a portion of which was sent to his mother in Oklahoma. When questioned by the police, she admitted that only eight dollars of the money belonged to her and the rest of it had been Parker's.

Evans added that when Parker's life insurance policy had been taken out, he had only paid the first premium. Subsequent payments had been made by both Cooper and J.W. Gordon.

Finally, he noted, an examination of Parker's remains revealed that a fatal quantity of arsenic had been ingested into his system. His vital organs had been saturated with it, and the deadly poison had taken his life. The arsenic had been given to him, Evans told the jury, by Josephine Cooper.

Attorney J.R. Fitzgerald made the opening statements and conducted a defense on Cooper's behalf. He claimed that she had played no part in getting James Parker to take out a life insurance policy naming her as the beneficiary. The two of them were engaged to be married and had planned their wedding for the first of the year. It was Parker who wanted that fact to be kept a secret, which is why none of her friends or neighbors knew anything about it. They had planned to take a wedding trip to the Southwest, and even after Parker had become sick, Cooper was so certain he would recover that she bought him new shirts and underwear to take on their honeymoon.

Fitzgerald questioned the autopsy report that named arsenic as the cause of Parker's death. He had suffered a bad attack of the flu and sustained an injury at work a short time before he became fatally ill. Parker did not believe in doctors but did take a considerable quantity of medicine, which may have contributed to his death. To make matters worse, he had also been engaged in making home-brewed beer and "white mule," a hard, colorless whiskey, and he consumed great quantities of it. He spent much of his time, Cooper claimed, in a drunken state, which made it difficult for him to work and take care of chores around the house.

After Parker became increasingly ill, Cooper had called Dr. Dixon, whom she claimed believed Parker's sickness was caused by too much white mule. On the third day Parker was unable to get out of bed, Cooper claimed that she wanted to take him to the hospital, but he refused to go. Finally, she contacted physicians at the Wabash Hospital, who insisted that he be brought in immediately. But it was too late, she said, and he died. She insisted that she had been trying to get medical care for him the entire time that he was sick, but she said Parker told her that his illness was brought on by drinking too much and eating too much candy from the Wabash freight house. She had been trying to help Parker, her attorney insisted, so why would she have killed him?

Fitzgerald admitted that Cooper had done some foolish things in her relationship with Parker but added that Parker had done some foolish things himself. Cooper, however, had an excuse—she had the mind of a thirteen-year-old girl, he said. Just a few years before, she had been an inmate at an insane asylum as the result of an injury she had sustained. This is why she went along with Parker's idea to write the letters to Gordon about slipping the man some poison. The letters were all Parker's idea, Fitzgerald insisted. He had actually dictated them himself. He had always liked Gordon, although he didn't know Gordon was having an affair with his fiancée, and the "poison letters" had merely been a joke.

Spectators at the trial noted that the jury did not look convinced by this account.

Dr. R.C. Young, an intern at the Wabash Hospital, was the first witness called by the state. He testified that he was called to the Cooper home, and when he arrived, Parker's feet were cold and clammy, his heartbeat was erratic and his breathing was shallow and forced. He administered one-thirtieth of a grain of strychnine as a stimulant, but it had no effect. Parker died less than fifteen minutes later. The next day, his vital organs were removed and given to the sheriff to be sent to Chicago for analysis.

Dr. Ludwig Hekoven, professor of pathology at the Rush Medical College, stated that he found irritation in the organs that appeared to be caused by poison. His examination revealed no sign of any illnesses that might have contributed to Parker's death.

Dr. W.A. Dixon testified that he was called twice to see Parker, once on Wednesday and again on Friday, the day the man died. He said that Parker had been vomiting and complained of burning sensations throughout his chest and abdomen. Dixon said that he didn't know what had caused the vomiting and pain but admitted that it could have been the result of arsenic poisoning. He left some tablets to be dissolved in water and given to Parker when his stomach could retain any substance. They were supposed to stimulate the lining of his stomach. He also gave Parker a small amount of morphine for his pain.

Dixon called on Parker again on Friday, and that morning Cooper told him that she had given Parker some ice cream. Dixon told her not to give him anything else until his stomach had recovered from the irritation. That morning, Parker's feet were cold, his pulse weak and his temperature below normal. He said he told Cooper that Parker's condition was critical and that he should be taken to the hospital, but Cooper refused.

Dixon admitted that he was concerned about the situation. He knew that Cooper had been sent to an insane asylum several years before, and he was worried that she was not thinking clearly. He said that when he had first seen Parker, he had not considered poison to be the cause of his illness but rather a bad reaction to white mule. However, when asked, Parker denied drinking anything that day and said that the only thing he had eaten had been some tomatoes.

The state continued its parade of witnesses, calling Jennie Godwin, Haven Whitehouse, Amanda Ely and even J.W. Gordon, who insisted that while he had been involved with Cooper, he had not encouraged her to send the letters asking for poison, and he certainly never intended to comply with her requests.

The trial was over a few days later, and the jury only took three hours to return a guilty verdict. Cooper was sentenced to fourteen years in prison, and investigators were never able to connect her to the earlier deaths that took place in her home.

Josephine Cooper served eleven years of her sentence and was released early for good behavior in 1933. She moved to Bloomington soon after but was hardly settled before she was being questioned by police for having written threatening letters to an Indianapolis man named Abe Rosenthal. In her letters, she demanded that he send her $500. Cooper was arrested in Decatur and taken to Springfield to answer to the charges, since using the

Josephine Cooper's house was one of many old, ramshackle structures to be torn down on East King Street to make way for development in the late 1990s. It's unlikely that anyone who lived in the house toward the end knew the number of deaths that had occurred within its walls.

mail for criminal purposes was a federal offense. She pled guilty, and she was released on probation.

Josephine Cooper died at the age of seventy-seven in 1954. Official versions of her death remain unclear as to whether she jumped, or was pushed, from the window of the second-story apartment where she was living. The incident occurred during the early morning hours, and she died later that day from her injuries. She was never able to explain what had happened to her.

Cooper's death closed a page in history but left some unanswered questions behind. In addition to being Decatur's first murderess, was she also Decatur's first serial killer? Did she actually kill four people instead of just one? We will likely never know the truth.

MURDER IN THE GRAVEYARD

The murder of cemetery worker Melbourn Savage stunned the city in the spring of 1930. Savage was a caretaker employed at Greenwood Cemetery on the South Side of the city at the time he was murdered in the graveyard. There have been many questions raised in the years since about the unsavory aspects of Savage's character and whether or not they led to his death. No matter what happened, though, his killer was never caught.

Savage's murder was directly connected to a "hobo jungle" that had taken shape just outside of the cemetery grounds. This was an encampment where transients and small-time criminals slept and stayed. The railroad tracks passed close to this area, and it was convenient for the hoboes to hop a freight train from one town to the next. The police would be quick to point out after the murder that many of these men were of questionable character and often were on the run from the law. It's likely that Savage's killer was one of these drifters, but no one can say for sure, and to make matters more puzzling, Savage's own criminal ties may have also marked him for death.

On the morning of May 22, 1930, Savage went down to a hobo camp that had appeared overnight in the southeast corner of the cemetery. This was a common occurrence, as the proximity of the railroad line often forced the caretakers to run drifters out of the graveyard. Men who found the shacks and shanties in the already established camp to be full would often spread out their bedrolls among the cemetery's gravestones. The caretakers were then forced to run the hoboes out the next morning. Unfortunately, Savage ended up with four bullets in the back for his trouble, and he died a few hours later without regaining consciousness.

His body was found by Dave Waybright, another caretaker, who had heard the sound of four shots being fired and came to look. He discovered Savage's body some distance from the hobo camp, on the edge of one of the cemetery's gravel roads. He assumed Savage was already dead, so he ran to the office of the cemetery superintendent to summon the police. A couple named Mr. and Mrs. John Duffey was arriving at the cemetery at the same time, and they also heard the shots.

Although covered in blood and with bullets through both his brain and his abdomen, Savage was still alive. John Duffey, who followed the sound of the gunfire, found that Savage was still breathing, and he moved him under a shade tree to make him more comfortable. Duffey's wife ran to find cemetery superintendent Charles Braden, who summoned an ambulance to take Savage to St. Mary's Hospital. He died later that morning without regaining consciousness.

While there were no witnesses to the actual murder, there were a number of conflicting accounts of what happened just after it. According to Dave

Waybright, who had heard the shots and discovered the body, he had seen a man with a bundle under his arm running toward the Illinois Central Railroad tracks shortly after the shots were fired. He told police investigators that he was sure this had been a vagrant from the hobo camp who was angry with Savage for running him off. The man retaliated by shooting Savage in the back, and then he had fled.

Strangely, though, ambulance driver Roy Hudson told police officers that he had seen a different man as he was leaving the cemetery. This man was no vagrant and was very well dressed, although he also had a bundle under his arm. He was hurrying away from the scene in the opposite direction from the railroad tracks and was outside the cemetery gates. He had hailed a southbound automobile being driven by a young woman and had climbed inside. Investigators later found the car but found no weapon inside. The young man the car's owner had picked up was questioned, but the police were forced to let him go.

With nothing else to go on, police rounded up nine or ten homeless men for questioning. The working theory was that Savage had been murdered by

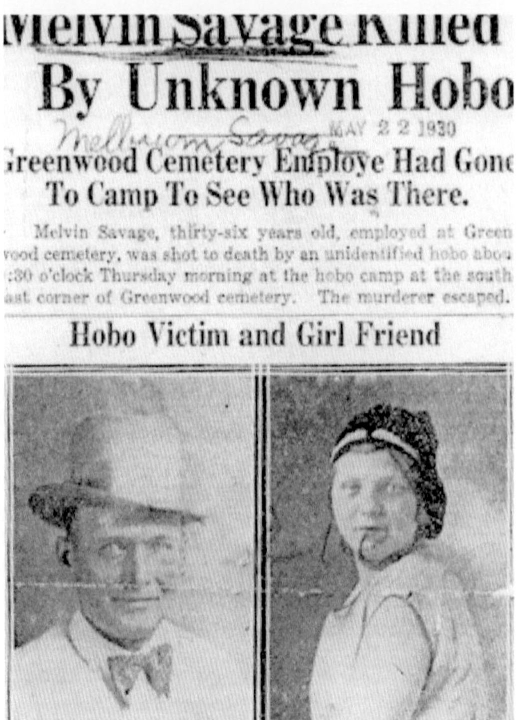

Melvin Savage Killed
By Unknown Hobo
MAY 22 1930
ireenwood Cemetery Employe Had Gone
To Camp To See Who Was There.

Melvin Savage, thirty-six years old, employed at Green vood cemetery, was shot to death by an unidentified hobo abou :30 o'clock Thursday morning at the hobo camp at the south ast corner of Greenwood cemetery. The murderer escaped.

Hobo Victim and Girl Friend

A newspaper clipping about the murder of Mel Savage in Greenwood Cemetery.

one of the men he had been rousting from the cemetery. Soon, however, the list of suspects grew.

Investigators began looking into Savage's past and began to find that he was not as well liked, or as reputable, as they first believed. He had been divorced in St. Louis three months prior to his death, and his ex-wife had filed charges against him for beating her. In addition, the police also found that Savage was possibly linked to organized crime in the St. Louis area. A number of letters found in his boardinghouse room on South Main Street were posted from St. Louis. His landlady said that whenever he was asked about the source of the letters, or his family, he always evaded answering the questions. It was also said that the caretaker often had more money than his salary would allow and that this spending cash may have come from valuables stolen at the cemetery. Savage was suspected of opening caskets before they were placed in the ground and helping himself to the contents. Firsthand testimony and sketchy evidence suggested that a local gang was robbing graves at Greenwood. Savage allegedly claimed, on more than one occasion, that he worked with this gang and that he sold jewelry and gold teeth to his criminal contacts in St. Louis.

Savage's personal life was also dubious. He was seeing a local girl at the time of this death. Her name was Sadie Lewis, and she was only sixteen years old. Savage, who was thirty-six, had represented himself as being ten years younger and had talked the girl's mother into letting him date her.

And it didn't stop there. Rumors in the neighborhood where he lived said that Savage had also been romantically involved with a number of married women and that one of their husbands had found out about the affair. Greenwood superintendent Charles Braden recalled that Savage had been badly beaten the winter before. He told his employer that he had been "ganged up on" by a group of men. Whether the beating had something to do with his extramarital affairs, or with the mysterious source of his extra cash, is unknown.

The suspect list was long and tangled, and the police were forced to hope that someone would come forward with information about the killer. A $300 reward was offered, but it was never claimed. Savage's killer simply vanished into thin air. Two months later, an inquest ruled that Melbourn Savage had been killed by "person or persons unknown." No mention was made of further suspects, and even though the case remained open, no further leads were ever discovered.

THE "HATCHET HOUSE" MURDERS

There is likely no murder case in Decatur's history that is as sensational as the Gambrill "Hatchet House" murders that took place in 1964. There is also no other case that is so seldom talked about. Younger people in Decatur have never heard of this startling, brutal and bloody set of murders, and the older people who remember the case rarely discuss it. It was an event that stunned the people of Decatur, and one that most would rather forget.

On the morning of March 2, 1964, the bodies of three members of a Decatur family were found hacked to death in their home on South Thirty-second Street. Everett L. Gambrill, age forty-nine; his wife, Mary, age forty-six; and their daughter, Anna Belle, age thirteen, were all found in their beds, likely murdered in their sleep. All had been attacked with an instrument identified by Police Chief James H. May as a hatchet, or hand axe.

The bodies were discovered at 9:30 a.m. by the Reverend David McConauhy and Patrolman John Corley. McConauhy, pastor of the Woodlawn Chapel Presbyterian Church, said that he had been contacted when Everett Gambrill had not shown up for work at Enterprise School, located a short distance from his home on South Country Club Road. Ordinarily, Gambrill arrived for work as a custodian at the school at 7:00 a.m. When he did not show up, the school office tried to telephone his home. After not receiving an answer, Gerald Weatherford, a fifth-grade teacher, and William Spencer, a substitute custodian, drove to the Gambrill residence. The two men returned to the school and notified the police.

McConauhy learned that Gambrill had not shown up for work and became worried. He had also not come to the church on Saturday afternoon, where he also worked, and the family had not attended Sunday services, which was unusual. He offered to accompany Officer Corley to the house, and when they went inside, they made the gruesome discovery. Mrs. Gambrill and her daughter had been slain in one bed, and Mr. Gambrill was found in a different room of the house.

Technicians from the state crime laboratory were brought in to assist in the investigation, and officers roped off the house and began speaking to the neighbors. Frances Romack, who lived nearby, said that she had not seen the family around the house all weekend. Another neighbor, Ed Bartosch, agreed and added that the house appeared to have been closed up. The police would soon learn that the Gambrills had been killed on Friday night and left in their blood-soaked beds until Monday morning.

Chief May told reporters that a motive in the murders had not been determined, but he emphasized that the police had a strong lead. He wouldn't elaborate on the statement, but what he wasn't telling the press soon became clear.

On Tuesday, March 3, the killer's name was revealed: Michael Gambrill, the son and brother of the murder victims. Gambrill, absent without leave from the Marine Corps, was arrested in Boynton Beach, Florida, on March 2 and admitted to killing his family. He had fled to Florida on Friday night after the killings. He told authorities in Florida that he wasn't sure why he became enraged enough to murder his family. Ordinarily, he was reported to have said that the only time he became excited was when he listened to bongo records. "And I wasn't playing bongo records when I was home," Gambrill said.

He was picked up almost by accident. He had been walking along U.S. 1 about 9:30 p.m. and was stopped by Police Sergeant William Hamilton and questioned. Gambrill said that he was a marine but failed to show his leave

Detectives outside of the Gambrill murder scene, which was dubbed the "Hatchet House."

papers and was taken to jail. While sitting in police headquarters, he blurted out a confession that he had slain his parents and his sister at their home in Decatur. Officers immediately notified the Decatur police, and Gambrill was held until Decatur detectives could arrive to bring him back to Illinois.

Two Decatur detectives, Sergeant Dale Schawitsch and Harold Miller, along with Glenn O. Fuller, assistant state's attorney, flew to Miami. They were taken to West Palm Beach, where Gambrill was being held, to take statements from him. Three murder warrants had been filed in Decatur against the young man. They were based on evidence that was recovered at the scene of the crime, including a cigarette lighter with the initials "M.G." that had been found in the yard.

"I'm very, very sorry. My parents were always nice to me," Gambrill said during his statements. The eighteen-year-old sobbed as he spoke of the events leading to the slaying of his family. Gambrill, a private first class in the Marine Corps, said that he left his base in San Diego because he wanted to come home and plead with his parents to allow him to get a British passport. He had asked them repeatedly by mail to get him the passport so that he could return to Ireland. His father had been in the service there and had married an Irish girl. Michael was born in Lytham, England. He wanted to get out of the Marine Corps and saw this as a way to do it, but his father objected.

Gambrill was very dissatisfied with his time in the Marine Corps. He had enlisted in September 1963 and went to boot camp in San Diego. He was then assigned to Camp Pendleton for infantry training and later reassigned to San Diego for training in the communications and electronics school. He later dropped out of the school for academic reasons and was given temporary duty in the mess hall. He went absent without leave on February 24 and returned to Decatur to plead his case for the passport once again. Gambrill fared no better arguing with his parents after he returned home.

On the Friday night of the murder, his family went to bed about 11:00 p.m. He told his parents that he wanted to stay up and watch a horror movie on television. When the movie was over, he started to go to bed, but standing there in the darkness, the emotions that he had apparently suppressed for most of his life finally boiled out of control, triggering a flash of real-life violence that was far worse than anything he had watched on television and ending in a bloodbath that sickened the police officers who discovered it a few days later.

He went down to the basement of the small frame house and came back upstairs with a hatchet. He walked into the front bedroom, where his mother and sister were sleeping. Anna Belle, who was deaf and had cerebral palsy, had been sick and was sleeping in her parents' bed with her mother. Gambrill killed his mother first and then his sister, slaughtering them both as they slept. Then he went into the back bedroom and killed his father, hitting him repeatedly with the blade of the hatchet. Covered in his family's blood, Gambrill sat in the living room before cleaning himself up and going out to the garage, where his father kept his 1958 Rambler. He climbed into the car and never looked back, driving for eighteen hours to Florida.

Gambrill told the detectives that he felt terrible about what he had done and decided to commit suicide. He purchased sleeping pills in a drugstore and swallowed ten of them, hoping that they would kill him. But he awoke the next morning with a terrible headache instead. He got dressed and drove the car south to Fort Pierce, ending up with a flat tire on the side of U.S. 1. He discovered that there was no spare tire in the car, so he decided to hitchhike south. He rode in three separate cars before he made it to Boynton Beach. He stopped to talk to a bridge tender, who warned him that he shouldn't be walking the streets at night because the police might pick him up. The man kindly gave him $1.50 for bus fare, and Gambrill was waiting for a bus when Sergeant William Hamilton picked him up. Once at the police station, Gambrill fell apart and confessed to the murders.

Gambrill waived extradition from Florida, and arrangements were made to bring him back to Illinois, but not before the San Diego police contacted West Palm Beach authorities about another murder. After Gambrill's arrest made newspaper headlines, the police in San Diego wanted him questioned about a murder that had taken place there on February 5. A young Alabama serviceman and his wife had been honeymooning in the city and had been shot to death in their beds in the middle of the night. With Gambrill in San Diego at the time, the police thought the murders were similar enough to the Decatur killings to warrant a few questions. He denied any involvement in the San Diego murders, and he was later ruled out as a suspect.

Two days later, Michael Gambrill was back in Decatur. The detectives had flown him back to Indianapolis, where they were met by an unmarked police car that drove them to Decatur. Gambrill's face was set as he walked through a group of reporters and photographers when he reached the Macon County Jail. He was clad in corduroy pants, a sports shirt and black suede shoes, which he exchanged for a set of jailhouse coveralls and slippers.

While funeral services were being held for his parents and sister at the Dawson & Wikoff Funeral Home, Gambrill was being photographed and fingerprinted at the jail. A half hour later, he was taken before magistrate

James R. Palmer, who explained his rights, and Gambrill entered pleas of not guilty to the three murder charges against him. The not guilty pleas were mandatory, since Palmer did not have the authority to accept a guilty plea on a murder charge. He ordered Gambrill to be held without bond. The state was represented during the arraignment by state's attorney Basil Greanias, although Gambrill did not yet have an attorney. A public defender was appointed for him a short time later.

First on the agenda for Gambrill was a mental competency exam, which was used to determine further action in his case. If judged to be legally sane, he would be prosecuted on one or more of the murder charges that had been filed against him. If doctors believed he was insane at the time of the killing, he would be sent to the Illinois Security Hospital at Menard Prison. He was taken to Springfield for his mental exams, and reports from the state doctors showed that he was legally sane. Plans were made to present Gambrill's case to the grand jury on April 6, when Greanias felt he would be indicted.

Soon after, Gambrill appeared for a preliminary hearing in front of magistrate Lester Brinkoetter, and public defender Albert E. Hurt was assigned to the young man's case. Brinkoetter ordered the hearing delayed for a week to give Gambrill time to discuss the charges with his attorney. Hurt later waived the hearing, action that was not opposed by Greanias, and said he saw no reason why the case would not go to trial as soon as possible. He also did not foresee any plans for a sanity hearing in regard to Gambrill's mental competency. Hurt was joined in his defense of Gambrill by Lloyd Lantendresse, a Decatur attorney and former prosecutor, and a trial date was set for May 18.

Gambrill appeared in court for his hearing in the custody of sheriff's deputy Paul Lichtenberger and was accompanied by his pastor, Reverend David McConauhy, who had discovered his family's bodies on the Monday after the murders. The pastor, as well as friends, former teachers and others associated with Gambrill, had recently been interviewed by the newspapers about the young man. McConauhy described him as "moody" but said that he didn't give any outward signs that he had a bad temper—or that he was going to kill his entire family. He had always believed that Gambrill had a rebellious streak and only attended church at his parent's insistence, but that streak disappeared after he joined the Marine Corps. Before leaving for boot camp, Gambrill often accompanied his father to work at the church on Saturday afternoons and frequently talked with the pastor. McConauhy described him as a boy who liked being alone and someone who would not reveal his true feelings.

Others agreed, and those who knew him stated that he was quiet and musically inclined. He had some problems in school, although none was serious, and he had always appeared to be an introverted student. His former principal at Eisenhower High School, Murvil Barnes, said Michael appeared to be a young person who lived in a shell and refused to be drawn into school activities.

Chief deputy sheriff Chris Vallas stated that Gambrill conducted himself as a model prisoner at the Macon County Jail, spending most of his time exercising in the common area and reading in his cell. His aunt from Indianapolis and uncle from Decatur brought him reading material on rock collecting and visited often, along with Reverend McConauhy. He didn't mix much with the other prisoners and spent most of his time by himself. Vallas said the young man was well behaved, but added that to his knowledge, he had never expressed any remorse about the hatchet slayings of his parents and sister.

Whether or not he expressed remorse, something affected the mind of Michael Gambrill in the weeks that followed. On May 18, when his trial was scheduled to begin, a hearing was held instead. The hearing was to discuss the change of Gambrill's innocent plea to one of guilty for the murder of his sister. He had agreed to the plea on a single count of murder, which would shorten any sentence that he might have received for all three murders. After a meeting in the judge's chambers and a formal reading of charges in court, Gambrill's plea was changed to one of guilty. The indictments charging him with the murder of his father and mother were dismissed. After ensuring that Gambrill understood the nature of the charge and the penalty that could be imposed, he sentenced him to fifty to one hundred years in prison. "It is my opinion," Judge Morthland said, "that because of the nature of the crime, the defendant should not ever again be released into society."

Michael Gambrill stood while the sentence was passed and showed no emotion at the judge's words. He had received what the judge believed amounted to a life sentence in prison, and he didn't seem to care. This was puzzling, but not as puzzling as the fact that after all this, a motive for the murders still seemed unclear. Gambrill never told investigators why he killed his family, and he refused to provide a reason to the state doctors who examined him during his mental exams.

When assistant state's attorney Glenn Fuller asked if he had a reason for committing the murders, Gambrill simply replied, "No, not that I can think of."

Unrepentant killer Michael Gambrill was released from prison in 2005.

Doctors asked if he felt that it was wrong when he killed his parents and sister, and he told them, "I didn't really feel anything." He had told detectives in his first statement: "Then, all of the sudden, I don't know, I got the urge to kill them and I did." He took the hatchet to the bedroom where his mother and sister were sleeping. "I just started swinging with it. When I started, I couldn't stop."

Dr. Milton Baumann, a Springfield psychiatrist who examined Gambrill and filed a report with the court, said that Gambrill had a higher than average IQ and stated that he showed evidence of being psychotic at the time of the crime, although he certainly knew the difference between right and wrong. He was struck by the fact that Gambrill showed a total lack of remorse for his crimes.

Another psychiatrist, Dr. Melvin Seglin of Chicago, examined Gambrill but did not submit a report to the court. He was asked by a reporter after the sentencing whether a nineteen-year-old boy could learn to live with the fact that he killed his parents and sister.

"I think he already has," Dr. Seglin said.

Gambrill was sent to prison to serve out what Judge Morthland believed would be a life sentence, becoming eligible for parole after twenty years. He was turned down for decades but was finally released from the prison in Vienna, Illinois, on December 5, 2005.

BIBLIOGRAPHY

Anderson, Karen, and Dayle Cochran Irwin. *Decatur Business*. St. Louis: G. Bradley Publishing, 1995.

Banton, O.T. *Decatur, Illinois*. Decatur, IL: Macon County Historical Society, 1983.

———. *History of Macon County, Illinois*. Decatur, IL: Macon County Historical Society, 1976.

Brockway, Edith. *Antebellum Decatur, 1816–1860*. Decatur, IL: Decatur Genealogical Society, 1968.

Coleman, E.T. *History of Macon County*. Decatur, IL: Macon County Historical Society, 1929.

Davis, James E. *Frontier Illinois*. Bloomington: University of Indiana Press, 1998.

Fliege, Stu. *Tales and Trails of Illinois*. Urbana: University of Illinois Press, 2002.

Howard, Robert. *Illinois: History of the Prairie State*. Grand Rapids, MI: William B. Eerdmans Publishing, 1972.

Hughes, Linda Clark. *Tales of Old Decatur*. Decatur, IL: Decatur Genealogical Society, 1976.

Irwin, Dayle Cochran, and Karen Anderson. *Decatur Entertainment*. St. Louis: G. Bradley Publishing, 1997.

———. *Decatur: Serving Others*. St. Louis, MO: G. Bradley Publishing, 1998.

Meyer, Charlotte, Margaret Meyer, Ruye Mochel and Helen Beeson. *People & Places in Decatur, 1900–1929*. Decatur, IL: Zonta Club of Decatur, 1975–76.

Parrish, Randall. *Historic Illinois*. Chicago: A.C. McClurg & Co., 1905.
Taylor, Troy. *Haunted Decatur*. Decatur, IL: Whitechapel Press, 2009.

NEWSPAPERS

Decatur Bulletin-Sentinel
Decatur Daily Herald
Decatur Evening Bulletin
Decatur Herald & Review
Decatur Tribune

ABOUT THE AUTHOR

Troy Taylor is an occultist, supernatural historian, crime buff and author of more than eighty books about ghosts, hauntings, history, crime and the unexplained in America. He is also the owner of the American and Illinois Hauntings Tour companies. Born and raised in Illinois, he developed an interest in mysteries and "things that go bump in the night" at an early age and later channeled his interest into developing tours and writing about hauntings and crime from American history. Troy currently lives in Chicago's West Loop neighborhood.

Visit us at

www.historypress.net